• •

Leading in Hyper-Complexity:

A Practical Guide for Leaders

T0326613

Leading in Hyper-Complexity: A Practical Guide for Leaders

Line Jehle
Dr. Marcus Hildebrandt
Stefan Meister
with interviews with ten global leaders
Foreword by Susanne Seegers

First published in 2016 by Libri Publishing

ISBN: 978-1-909818-77-4

Cover design by Helen Taylor

Design by Carnegie Publishing

Libri Publishing
Brunel House
Volunteer Way
Faringdon
Oxfordshire
SN7 7YR

Tel: +44 (0)845 873 3837

www.libripublishing.co.uk

Table of Contents

List of Figures, Tables, Text boxes and Exhibits

Figures

Tables

Textboxes

Exhibits

Acknowledgments

We thank Susanne Seegers for writing the foreword to our book within a very short time frame.

We are very grateful to those leaders who were willing to go through the interview process with us in this highly new field where little good practice is known so far:

Patricia Anthony, Leandro Baghdadi, Dr. Christian Ecke, Javier Escobedo, Luis Pedro Ferreira, Stephen Karnik, Arnulf Keese, Dr. Armin Klesing, Xavier Randretsa, and Chunhu Wang.

We thank Susanne Skoruppa for her contribution to this book.

We thank Anette Grimmelsmann for her support and her patience with the three authors.

We thank Frank Jehle for his legal advice and moral support.

We thank intercultures' Berlin office for transcription assistance and proofreading.

We further thank Laurence Baltzer, Dr. Anja Grosch and Jobst Scheuermann for reading through the draft of the book and giving us feedback.

We thank Tilo Schneider for designing and producing the great icons that make navigating this book easier.

Why three names on the title page? Here is an overview of our different roles and responsibilities:

- Line and Marcus created the content of the book.

- Marcus was responsible for the images.

- Line and Stefan recruited interview partners; Stefan processed the interviews in part three of the book.

- Stefan provided valuable feedback and enriched the book with intercultural aspects.

Foreword

Working in today's global businesses – whatever your specialization – isn't easy. Dealing with complexity is one of the most challenging issues facing modern business and complexity is being widely acknowledged as one of the biggest barriers to success.

Chances are, if you have picked up this book, that you are facing the many challenges of managing and delivering results in increasingly complex work settings and that you have decided to take action.

Whether you are already an experienced manager or new to the field, you have come to the right place.

This book is about giving you the knowledge and tools necessary to be a successful manager in a hyper-complex organization. It will give you an insight into complexity, its nature and causes and will enable you as a manager to get on top of complexity and develop strategies to work and bring results in a hyper-complex environment.

As a human resources professional, I have worked in the public and private sector and I have experienced how complexity has increased over the years to today's hyper-complex, network-based and multi-cultural organizations.

There are many differences between public organizations and private corporations, but when it comes to developing the competencies, skills and abilities of employees, in my experience, they have much more in common than what separates them. Whether driven by profit or other objectives, whether accountable to owners or the public through government officials, every organization wants success. And success, ultimately, is all about people and their ability to perform. And as complexity increases, the success of any organization, public or private, often stands and falls by whether its managers are able to successfully and professionally navigate the organization through the myriad of obstacles it is facing.

I have worked for several international organizations and whether these organizations were implementing military aspects of a peace agreement, opening up roads, repairing or replacing bridges, freeing up airports and railway lines in war-torn countries or developing international trade or – as my current work place – helping end impunity for the perpetrators of the most serious crimes, I have as an HR professional always been facing the same key challenges, namely: how to enable employees to make meaningful contributions and how to create a sense of purpose and belonging.

Few things are more rewarding and motivating than a job well done and employees who feel competent and appreciated produce more. It's that simple, yet that difficult. Whether private industry or public administration, many if not most organizations are struggling with the challenges of managing complexity. To succeed as an organization and as individuals, it is critical that managers learn to deal with and gain a sense of control over their complex working environments. By reading this book, you have taken a significant step towards becoming such a manager.

This book, its authors and its subject are especially significant to me because of the years I have spent helping recruiting what we believed were the best and most competent managers – just to see that too many subsequently would struggle finding their place and operating in the complicated and intricate environment an international organization has to offer. As a result, I am passionate about how we best enable and support managers at all levels in the organizations to live out their potential and perform successfully.

I have known Line Jehle for many years and long admired her pioneering work in the area of cross-cultural competencies and the ability of organizations to collaborate across distances and differences. With thoughtfulness, insight and humour, she has trained and developed managers at all levels to improve organizations' ability to handle complexity. Also the work of Dr. Marcus Hildebrandt and Stefan Meister in the field of developing global cultures of collaboration has impressed me. Together they form a dynamic and top-notch team with an unparalleled expertise in how to manage in complexity. With this book, they have combined their knowledge into one useful tool. The book is enriched with an exquisite collection of interviews with leaders in globally operating organizations who share their thoughts and useful and interesting experience.

Just like their first book "Closeness at a Distance" which has been described as "a groundbreaking approach to the challenges so many teams, and team leaders, face today", this book will change the way we as managers deal with complexity. More than that, it delivers on the promise to teach managers how to take control and be "Leading in Hyper-Complexity" anytime and anywhere!

I hope you too will enjoy the journey Dr. Hildebrandt, Line Jehle, Stefan Meister and "Leading in Hyper-Complexity" take you on.

Susanne Seegers
Chief of the Human Resources Section
International Criminal Court, The Hague
47 years old, married, two children

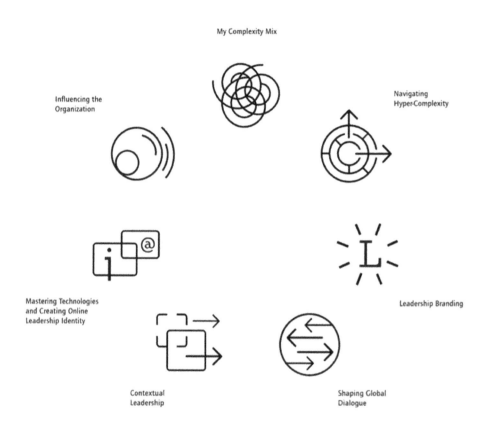

Figure i: Hyper-complexity

"A great person attracts great people and knows how to hold them together." Johann Wolfgang von Goethe

● ●

Introduction

Meet Paul. Paul works for a global company that is part matrix* organization, part network. He leads a group consisting of several teams whose members are spread across three continents: Europe, Asia and the United States. He is a mature manager in his early forties, experienced in running large projects and handling substantial budgets. So far, he has mainly worked with one team at a time. As his company has been evolving from the typical matrix structure to a network organization, Paul's work has largely shifted to leading virtual groups. He has adopted his mindset accordingly.

However, many of his colleagues still believe that they are working in a matrix organization, albeit a very complicated one with three or four dimensions. They try to steer this system with the rational methods they have used so far. They are not aware that part of their work context has shifted to a network or community environment with a different underlying dynamic. In consequence, they are becoming increasingly frustrated because they are no longer able to control the system.

---

* A matrix describes a tableau that consists of horizontal rows and vertical columns. An employee in a matrix organization typically reports on their day-to-day performance to the project or product manager whose authority flows sideways (horizontally) across departmental boundaries. They also report on their overall performance to the head of their department whose authority flows downwards (vertically) within the department.

Today is a Bank Holiday and Paul is taking a walk in his local park. The simplicity of being outside makes him realize once more that his job is becoming more and more complex. He enjoys leading virtual groups, enjoys the characteristic juggling of working with different teams and tasks simultaneously. From the interaction of the international and cultural diversity of his colleagues very creative solutions have emerged that have earned much attention and praise from senior management.

But working and networking virtually can also be exhausting. He is often struggling to combine the global goals of the company with the local realities of the team members. Culture, language, time zones, power distribution or access to information are just some of the topics that require continuous balancing. Tasked with juggling these seemingly conflicting needs, delivering results can sometimes be difficult.

Standard approaches to problem solving and to leading no longer work in the virtual world. Naturally, it's impossible to constantly control and understand what's going on with team members in other parts of the world. And frankly, Paul sometimes wishes that the kind of personal, face-to-face connection of his local team, which feels a bit like family, could be extended to his global network.

These challenges often force Paul out of his comfort zone. He feels that being a virtual team leader is a two-edged sword, heightening the excitement of work but also increasing its complexity.

Paul's challenges represent the reality of many managers and members of organizations that work globally and virtually (meaning cross-location and/or cross-border). The increasing complexity of our globalized work environments has changed the context of basic human needs in organizations. These include:

- The sense of belonging to the organization and its members.

- The need for understanding and influencing the organization.

- The need for developing and learning with the organization.

An organization has to satisfy these needs if it wants to retain its people and enable them to make successful contributions and, in turn, to reinforce the organizational sense-making processes. Moreover, these three principles are strongly related to the basic human desire to reduce the complexity created by the objects surrounding the individual human being. It is about the eternal desire to control and manage or at least to deal and cope with complexity.

But even this complexity has evolved to a new level which we call "hyper-complexity" (see Part IV: The concepts of complexity and hyper-complexity). Hyper-complexity denotes different layers of complexity such as social interactions in an intercultural environment, new technological means of communication, organizational dynamics or market dynamics, which, through being linked, lead to new emerging patterns.

In hyper-complex environments, satisfying the basic human needs introduced above requires a radically different approach. Belonging is suddenly no longer linked to a shared physical space, and time stretches over temporal and geographical distances and becomes part of the dynamic, as does learning. Similarly, influence is exerted without being physically present with one's team members.

The purpose of this book

This book is written for the global, virtual manager who is faced with the challenge of managing hyper-complexity that is so characteristic of global networked collaboration. Leadership paradigms have been changing dramatically in the recent past. As the traditional local organization and the classical team configuration are quickly becoming relics of the past, effective leadership requires radically different approaches. Among many other tasks, the successful manager is evaluated based on her* ability to succeed in the face of growing and linked sources of complexity.

This book aims to equip experienced managers with the knowledge and the tools necessary to accomplish this task. In Part II, we will take you on a learning journey through the following topics:

- Navigating hyper-complexity (p. 39): You will learn how to cope with the unknown in your professional life.

- Leadership branding (p. 65): You will learn how to develop your unique and authentic leadership brand that attracts followers.

- Contextual leadership (p. 93): You will learn about the ability to analyze your work context in order to be able to choose the corresponding leadership approaches that best fit that specific context.

- Mastering technologies and creating online leadership identity (p. 122): You will understand the importance of mastering the communication technology in successful leadership and what one has to

---

* Throughout this book, we will express our appreciation of gender diversity by using masculine and feminine pronouns interchangeably.

take care of, and you learn what it takes to fine tune your leadership online identity in order to make an impact on your co-workers also in the virtual world.

- Shaping global dialogue (p. 157): You will learn how important it is to create a voicing/feedback culture and how this can be done in a smart way.

- Influencing the organization (p. 194): You will get to know the levers for changing an organization on a larger scale and will learn how to take care of the inner dynamics and the framework of a system in order to achieve sustained changes within the organization.

This book complements the knowledge presented in our previous book "Closeness at a Distance: Leading Virtual Groups to High Performance". In "Closeness at a Distance" we introduced key concepts for reducing the complexity of global cooperation, including *Virtual Closeness* and *Purple Space*. We also wrote about the Virtual Performance Assessment and the corresponding process of Virtual Performance Improvement, two key elements of a framework for improving the performance of virtual groups, teams and networks. We have included some of the concepts of "Closeness at a Distance" in Part IV of this book.

Now our aim is to show managers how these concepts translate into leading themselves, others and the organization effectively in the face of hyper-complexity through:

- Purpose-oriented Purple Spaces: how to align organizational needs with global cooperation spaces?

- Leadership and Virtual Closeness: how to influence hyper-complex environments as a leader?

The structure of this book

This book is written for practitioners. Its focus is on practical concepts and tools that can be implemented directly.

It is divided into three parts. We have devised icons that will help the reader navigate the book.

Figure ii: Icon: Identifying your complexity mix

In Part I, "Identifying your complexity mix", we lay the theoretical groundwork by defining the three types or forms of organizational contexts found in different compositions in contemporary business: family, machine and network.

We will also take a closer look at the concept of complexity and its corresponding degrees in each organizational form. At the end of the first part, we will offer the reader a self-assessment based on a set of indicators to determine in which organizational form and corresponding degree of hyper-complexity he is currently operating.

In Part II, "Dealing with your complexity mix", we introduce six central areas of leading in the face of hyper-complexity. While these areas are not exhaustive and there are many other aspects to take into account, we believe that understanding and mastering them will equip the reader with the knowledge and tools necessary to lead effectively in global hyper-complexity. For each of these six areas, we suggest concrete interventions the reader can practice and implement directly with his group, team or network community. These areas include:

Figure iii: Icons: Navigating hyper-complexity; Leadership branding; Contextual leadership; Mastering technologies and creating online leadership identity; Shaping global dialogue; Influencing the organization

Navigating hyper-complexity

Leadership branding

Contextual leadership

Mastering technologies and creating online leadership identity

Shaping global dialogue

Influencing the organization

Part III, "Personal mixes and recipes", is a collection of interviews with leaders in globally operating organizations whom we asked how they perceive their work context and how they deal with hyper-complexity. These interviews serve two purposes. First, they provide real-life validation of the theory we develop in the book. And second, due to the uniform set of practical questions we asked our interviewees, they present case studies of good leadership practice in network organizations.

Part IV, "Deeper into the mix", is devoted to those readers who would like to gain a deeper insight into the background of our approaches. It is a collection of short texts concerning different topics of the book that represents our deeper and not yet consolidated reasoning in these areas. These texts represent work in progress.

How to read this book

We have written this book in the style of a workbook. Depending on your needs and interests, you may want to focus only on selected topics and interviews in Parts II and III. Throughout the book, a sidebar navigation with central messages and the icons we have introduced above enable quick scanning and selective reading.

While the structure of the book follows a logical sequence and can be read from front to back, it is also written in a way that allows jumping between topics, especially in Part II. It is not necessary to read through the six chapters sequentially. Rather, they are all self-contained chapters that can be picked and chosen from according to the individual reader's needs and interests.

Part I: Identifying your complexity mix

One of the most urgent realizations today is that environmental changes are accelerating and interlinked through networks. This applies to nature as well as to the business world and both worlds are coupled in a non-linear way. The ensuing paradigm shifts can be embodied in one question.

What is the difference between complicated and complex? Here is an ambitious answer:

- Complicated: if you think and analyze hard enough, you'll find the answer and you can predict things.

- Complex: you can look at parts of the system but will never be able to fully analyze the system. A bit like the weather: you can hope and partly predict it but you can't guarantee it.

The difference between complicated and complex

A complex system is characterized by two elements:

- The principle impossibility to describe precisely the state or level of its constituting elements, and, as a consequence of that,

- The unpredictability of its future development.

Complex systems are unpredictable

In consequence, we can never accurately predict the behaviour of a complex system when interacting with it.

9

Its reaction can come as a complete surprise (e.g. in form of the butterfly effect[*]) or it can indeed adhere to linear steering principles of cause and effect (e.g. in form of the so-called enslaving principle[†] – even though this may not be the best terminology for a physical principle) in spite of its complexity. We can never know in advance which of these reactions will occur (see Part IV: "The concepts of complexity and hyper-complexity", p. 266 for further information on this). Social networks and communities are complex systems, and are a reality of our business world (see Part IV: "The concepts of groups, networks and communities, p. 269, for further information on this).

As we can never be fully prepared for the things to come in these contexts, we need to learn how to deal with the unknown professionally. This is the new normality of our interconnected working lives. The good news is that there will always be things known and familiar to us.

In the interview with Leandro Baghdadi (p. 233), Leandro nicely shows how great complexity exists even within one region, Latin America, where different time zones, the different versions of Spanish spoken (not to forget Portuguese), and what he calls the Latin American "sense of urgency" are familiar elements that never cease to create unexpected and complex situations to deal with.

It is this mixture of well-known elements and new territory of organizational contexts which we will discuss here. Reading the following pages will enable you to analyze and manage your own context, as far as its complexity will allow.

---

[*]   The butterfly effect posits that small changes in a system can have a strong impact on the system's future state.

[†]   The enslaving principle is used to reduce the complexity of a system by forcing all elements of the system to align. It was introduced by the physicist Hermann Haken; Haken (1983).

The three forms of organization

In our work and research we have identified three elementary organizational forms. All of them can exist simultaneously, and all internationally active organizations have features of all three. However, they differ in the mixture of these three elementary forms on the global and local level. While local management may be structured like a family, the shop floor can look like a machine, and global distribution may function as a network or community. The point of this classification is not to suggest that any one organization is either or, but rather, to show that all or at least two of these organizational forms are likely to exist simultaneously within one organization. None of them is better or worse than the other. Rather, they serve different purposes within an organization. While all of the global leaders we interviewed for this book confirm this co-existence, Stephen Karnik (Part III, p. 222) describes the co-existence of family and network parts in a global non-profit organization particularly well.

Family, machine and network

The classification "family, machine, network/community" also denotes the historical development of organizing[*]. While the family provided the sole organizational form for centuries (and maybe longer), industrialization introduced the idea of the machine that runs smoothly based on scientific knowledge and efficiency. The recent knowledge and idea revolutions, fuelled by globalization, have been bringing the network and the community configurations to the forefront of today's organizations.

Never during this development was a whole organizational code overwritten by the new algorithm of organizing. Rather, new forms emerge in certain parts of the organization and overlap with older structures. Similarly, this

---

[*]   Eva Roettgers-Ferchland introduced Marcus Hildebrandt to this concept in a training; Roettgers-Ferchland (2008).

development can be traced within the history of individual organizations. While an organization may have started out as a family structure (like most start-ups do), it will grow to a machine-like structure as processes and structures are increasingly needed to consolidate and standardize the results of the growth. And as the machine globalizes its reach, it typically turns, in whole or in part, into a network or community structure. This development can happen sequentially (i.e. historically) or simultaneously, both throughout the whole organization and in single parts.

How is this connected to complexity?

Complexity within organizations is determined by the following sources:

- The complexity of an individual human being (e.g. values, needs, emotional states, mental models, competences, motivation, etc.).

- The complexity of the interactions between human beings (behaviours, reactions, etc.).

- The complexity of the non-human elements and their interactive dynamics both inside of and with the environment of the organization (structures, processes, tangible and intangible assets, shares, customers, competitors, society, etc.).

Each of these organizational contexts contains a mechanism to reduce complexity and is therefore attractive and stable for its members for very specific reasons

The degree of complexity and its sources can vary from one organizational context to another, depending on the composition of these three sources.

Connecting what we have set out so far, we believe that the existence of the three organizational contexts family, machine and network is interconnected with the notion of complexity. This is because each of these organizational contexts contains a mechanism to reduce complexity and is therefore attractive and stable for its members for very specific reasons.

Here are some examples of organizational contexts that we have observed and that show some kind of generic pattern.

Organizational forms overlap and co-exist

- Think of the manager of a local branch of a large bank or retail-chain. Fluctuation among the 3–8 local staff is low. They have developed a strong relationship with each other and the local manager. They feel and behave like family. However, corporate controlling is centralized and ensures that the local branches achieve the company goals and that the global strategy is implemented locally. There may also be other centrally organized processes such as procurement and logistics. This is the machine side of the local organization. The local manager may participate in a global corporate knowledge exchange or personal development network to keep up with the relevant global processes. However, the machine and network parts are less prevalent in the day-to-day compared to the family part.

- Imagine a manager of a production line at an automotive company. Saving costs as well as managing for efficiency and quality are the main leadership tasks in this context. Ideally, things should run smoothly like a "machine". However the local production technology and the corresponding knowledge stem from a global innovation network. Local management has to ensure that the engineers at the production site contribute to, and profit from, this global knowledge basis. Also, in spite of the fact that headcount is mainly a cost factor, personal leadership based on local relationships is an important success factor for local efficiency. Employees' motivation to support continuous improvement processes relies strongly on their personal identification with the quality of the local processes and structures as well as long-term opportunities for learning and advancing within the organization.

13

In this scenario, the machine format is the dominating organizational form, with elements of family and network.

- Consider a leader in a global IT company. Her team consists mainly of knowledge workers who are spread across the globe. Innovation and flexibility are key for success in this rapidly evolving environment. Therefore, the leader's core task is to create and influence purpose driven communities and networks. However, the leader also has to provide family-like structures and processes to create a sense of belonging for the network members. Moreover, certain processes have to be standardized, especially parts of the software development processes and customer services. Not an easy thing to achieve in this rather fluid organization, but also an important success factor for sustained growth. This reflects the machine element of the network organization.

The predominant organizational form exerts power

Crucially, the predominant organizational form exerts power and change is therefore difficult. When initiating change, leaders ought to be able to assess the status quo correctly and communicate clearly what the purpose of the organizational change is, and towards which organizational structural mix they had best move.

We believe that any healthy and long-living organization should always have a purpose driven mix of all three of those organizational contexts. If this is not the case the organization is much less likely to address and process the complexity of its environment. In consequence, it loses long-term attractiveness for employees and customers as well as its ability to compete in the market.

Rivalry

However, these systems can also be rivals. For example, the machine system can have difficulties interfacing with the network because of the lack of structure and processes in the latter.

The same can happen between the family and the machine. In the family structure, the relationship has a higher priority than the process. This can cause the family to bend the rules (i.e. the processes) to serve the relationships.

Your ability as a leader to assess and manage the context in which you are operating is therefore essential. The chapter "Contextual leadership" (p. 93) is devoted to the details of how to practise such contextual leadership. But for now, let's take a closer look at the three organizational contexts to answer the following questions.

- What are the sources and composition of complexity?

- How is complexity reduced within a given context?

- What makes the context attractive for its members in the three needs categories?
  - The need to belong to the organization and its members.
  - The need to understand and influence the organization.
  - The need to develop and learn with the organization.
- Which factors play an important role in leadership initiatives?

Here is a brief summary for those readers who don't intend to go into too much detail on this.

- **Family**: **human complexity** → This complexity stems from the unpredictable dynamics of holistic human interaction and is reduced by the strong social fabric.

- **Machine**: **process complexity** → This complexity results from more structures, from technology and from the higher number of employees. It is reduced by clearer definitions of roles and functions that

Sources and degrees of organizational complexity and the mechanisms to reduce it

lead to a less strong social fabric (I can still work with a person I don't like).

- **Network/community**: **pattern complexity** → This complexity results from the dynamic nature of networks and communities and their fluidity. It is reduced by a shared purpose, shared behaviours and other principles of attractiveness. Because most of this happens virtually, this complexity sees the lowest density of social fabric (If I don't like someone I can virtually disappear).

The parallelism and interconnection of these different organizational forms makes contemporary organizational contexts hyper-complex (see Part IV: "The concepts of complexity and hyper-complexity", p. 266, for further information on this).

The following is a more detailed account of this brief summary.

Organizational contexts and their sources of complexity: Family, machine and network/community

The family-like context: Human complexity

Like in a healthy and prospering family, this type of organizational context is built on strong face-to-face relationships and relies on leadership based on authority and care for the wellbeing of its employees. Learning is based on education or instruction through direct contact with the superiors or more experienced members of the organization. As fluctuation is low, people arrange themselves with colleagues and fight for their niche. This context is predominant in organizations with a high number of small autonomous sites or affiliates. Organizational units are aligned by a central strategy and supported by central processes (logistics, corporate communication, marketing, procurement, etc.).

Sources and composition of complexity

- The way employees are treated reflects the entirety of their human complexity including very personal values, needs, emotional states, mental models, competences, motivation, family, relatives, biography, etc. The approach to individual interaction takes into account all these aspects in a holistic way.

- Only few structures and standardized processes exist, and they often grew organically over long periods of time. Rules and patterns of activities tend to be very clear and fixed.

- The complexity of the organization equals the complexity of the human beings who work there.

- Every member can be a direct source of interaction with the environment. In most cases, there are no central filters for relevant information coming from the outside.

How complexity is reduced

- The number of members is kept small. The aim is for long-term and intensive, holistic relationships.

- Role concepts are few, vague, and rather implicit.

- Sometimes, external influence is only perceived as marginally relevant for changing the organization.

- The speed of change can be rather slow.

What makes this context attractive for its members

- The values lived by the founding members or the "parents" (heads) of the "family" provide a stable organization, which enables members to develop a strong sense of belonging.

- The organization can be understood and steered by the few existing and roughly described roles of the few members and through personal and face-to-face-based relationship management (understanding and influencing the organization).

- Personal development comes primarily from learning on the behavioural and psychological levels, based on spontaneous and situational feedback. A useful method for this is Peer Group Consulting, which focuses on the full complexity of human relations in interactions (developing and learning within the organization).

Factors that tend to play an important role in leadership initiatives

- A strong feeling of personal closeness between employees and leaders is created.

- Simple and clear answers to bottom-up questions like "what to do?" and "where to go?" are provided.

- Learning is facilitated through instructional approaches by the traditional role of an educator or a teacher.

- Influences from the environment that are not relevant for the organization's development are filtered or blocked.

The machine-like context: Process complexity

With increasing market pressure on the cost level, organizations put more emphasis on efficiency and cost reduction. A typical example of this trend is the automotive industry, but any other manufacturing companies that produce objects consisting of a large number of pieces often show the same characteristic features. They need to design and standardize core procedures and align processes across the organization in order to increase productivity. The same can often be observed in companies that have undergone a period of significant growth. They are then faced with the task of consolidating the results of organic or even explosive growth processes into newly designed structures in order to reduce the augmented complexity in the organization.

It is this desire to bring the organization into a controllable format of smooth and efficient processes that coins the "machine" terminology for this type of organization.*

Sources and composition of complexity

- The machine is characterized by a multitude of carefully designed structures and processes that span the whole organization.

- Large numbers of employees in this organizational form entail a large number of interfaces that need to be managed.

- Moreover, there are a lot of interactions with the environment that have to be filtered, analyzed and made sense of.

How complexity is reduced

- The function-based concept of "persona" (the Greek word for mask) with a detailed description of roles and responsibilities is introduced. Communication within the organization takes place between

---

* We would like to clarify that by using the term "machine", we do not suggest any negativity whatsoever attached to this organizational type. It clearly has distinct advantages and parts of an organization should always be designed in this way if the context so demands.

representatives of the different functions. Not all dimensions of human concern are taken into account when interacting and leading people.

- The organization is divided into smaller units (e.g. groups, teams, functional units, local organizational units).

- Rational standards for structures, processes and other constituting elements are defined. Complexity is further reduced by introducing HR functions, processes for the purpose of committing to organizational objectives, and through the attempt to create a corporate culture.

- Interaction with the environment is managed by introducing the function of external communication and the concept of corporate governance. External influences are analyzed and processed through creating and implementing strategies. This is supported by change management to orchestrate internal changes in a standardized way.

- Other business processes such as conflict management with institutionalized escalation systems are introduced.

- Concepts like process reengineering, core competences, total quality management and the like are established.

What makes this context attractive for its members

- Top management designs and works to implement corporate values, a strategy, a corporate culture and governance principles. These elements may be attractive to potential employees (sense of belonging).

- Due to the large degree of standardization and the corresponding degree of predictability the organization can deliver high quality products (understanding and influencing the organization).

- Employees can identify with these jointly created high-quality products; see, for example, the BMW automotive company, where employees' pride in their company is fuelled whenever a new product is presented to them first before its official market launch (sense of belonging).

- Employees belong to smaller organizational units (sense of belonging).

- Decisions are delegated to the appropriate level of competence (understanding and influencing the organization, developing and learning within the organization).

- Employees identify with the design of the organization (structures and processes) and use it to influence the organization (understanding and influencing the organization).

- Elaborate functional role concepts allow for separating of the professional persona from the private persona: I only "sell" the professional part of myself to the organization and keep private and intimate aspects of my life separate. This is reinforced through institutionalized feedback processes as part of the commitment to objective processes including professional and personal development (developing and learning within the organization). These functional role concepts work best in contexts where this separation is deeply embedded in national or regional culture, i.e. Germany, Switzerland and the Netherlands. It may also work for the profit of organizations with a much lesser degree of separation in cultures where the concept of "success" reaches from professional into the private, i.e. the US or, with slightly different definitions of success, in Japan or China, amongst other Asian cultures.

- Setting up a training and coaching system (developing and learning within the organization).

Factors that tend to play an important role in leadership initiatives

- The leaders of the organization design organizational principles, processes and structures that employees can identify with, thereby creating a form of (abstract) closeness to shared mental models.

- Employee development is led and supported using the roles and systems provided by HR (situational leadership and transformational leadership).

- The corporate strategy, values and governance principles are lived.

- Lean structures and business processes are designed and implemented.

- Weak signals* from the environment that might impact the competitive advantage of the organization are identified.

- An openness and ability to change.

- The framework for smooth global interactions is set.

Network and community-like contexts: Pattern complexity

Organizations that operate like networks or communities are often found in business areas that are mainly knowledge driven. In those environments, individual expertise plays a critical role, and there is a need for fast and radical innovation in the short run.

---

* Weak signals are not readily and easily recognizable among the majority of signals, either because they are not loud enough or they are simply different. They are absolutely needed if innovation is supposed to take place.

The large Internet companies are typical representatives of this organizational type. They were often born out of a network or community and rely significantly on self-organization and the collective knowledge of a network of experts.

Network-like organizations also tend to form naturally when start-ups don't have sufficient local expertise, aren't able to pay certain essential experts as full-time employees, or when larger companies form virtual organizations in order to bundle core competences of different organizations for the purpose of mastering complex customer demands. Read more on the specifics of networks and communities in Part IV ("The concepts of groups, networks and communities, p. 269).

Source and composition of complexity

- The number of members in this organizational form typically falls between the family and the machine.

- Its characteristic complexity is created by the fact that the organization is spread across a larger geographical sphere with fewer local members compared to family and machine.

- Moreover, the network tends to have fuzzy contours regarding membership. Customers, suppliers and sometimes even competitors as well as other outside stakeholders can be part of a network or a community. The network is therefore an open system in principle.

- The main organizational principle is the self-organization of experts within the corporate framework. In consequence, processes, roles and responsibilities are rather fluid, if they exist at all, and solidify temporarily only if demanded by the context. Agile software development processes within a network are a good example of this. Another example is virtual organizations that result from strategic alliances between different companies and that are based on a specific need. They typically process customer demands a single company could not manage.

+ Most communication is mediated by electronic systems and meeting face-to-face is an exception from the rule.

+ The principle of corporate volunteering becomes increasingly important on a larger scale. For example, people provide cross-functional support for a chance to do work beyond their routine and to find challenges that create a sense of purpose for them.

How complexity is reduced

+ A global netiquette and a shared purpose with which members can identify are introduced. Networks and communities centre on shared purposes. They live and strive on the development of shared behaviours. These processes have to be fostered by management.

+ Concentration is on influencing those elements or individuals of the network or community that are most influential (i.e. hubs), or on focusing on those resources within the network that provide new solutions to organizational challenges (especially weak links; see Part IV: "The concepts of groups, networks and communities, p. 269, for further information on this).

+ The internal dynamics and patterns of the organization (the organizational attractors) are identified and initiatives are built on those intrinsic force fields.*

---

* See the "Optimization-Polarity-Resonance" (OPR) approach by Scheuermann and Hildebrandt (2015).

- The principles of self-organization and self-similarity* are introduced and focus is on short-term deliverables (agile management).

- The environment is incorporated in the system through the active inclusion of relevant external perspectives.

- The individuals that personify the functions comprising the network or community are identified and cooperated with (see chapter "Contextual leadership").

What makes this context attractive for its members

- Attractive leaders (sense of belonging). Attractiveness in this context is defined by the extent to which group members want to be part of the discourse or the projects initiated or supported by a leader (see chapter "Leadership branding", p. 65).

- Autonomous self-organization processes (understanding and influencing the organization, developing and learning).

- Possibilities for informal and self-organized learning (developing and learning within the organization).

- The possibility to share perspectives and experiences globally (developing and learning within the organization).

- Developing innovative and creative solutions to existing problems in a short time frame (sense of belonging and understanding and influencing the organization).

---

* A self-similar system shows the same structures and shapes on all hierarchical levels, for example empowerment on individual, team and organizational levels. Alternatively, the whole has the same shape as one or more of the parts, such as a central structure in a team, a local and a global organization.

Factors that tend to play an important role in leadership initiatives

- Virtual closeness (sense of belonging; see Part IV: "Some concepts from "Closeness at a Distance", p. 296).

- The principles underlying attractiveness: reverse management, contextual leadership and leadership branding (see chapters "Leadership branding", p. 65 and "Contextual leadership", p. 93).

- Identifying weak signals that could turn into future attractors, and reinforcing them.

- Influencing hubs and weak links*.

- Creating an appropriate framework for self-organization and global sharing.

- Constant awareness of the voluntary nature of networks and communities and according behaviour.

Self-assessment: My complexity mix and the mix "of the other side" with whom I interact

In reality, there isn't just one clear mix of organizational elements that describe the context of a leader but rather a multitude of different ones existing in parallel. Depending on the corporate interface, in most cases your own context will be different from that of your customers' or from your co-workers' perceptions. As a leader, your task is to bridge the different worlds and/or adjust your approach accordingly (see also the interviews with Dr. Christian Ecke

---

* Weak links are connections that reach outside of one's regular contact group. The importance of weak links cannot be stressed enough as they enable us to reach out into completely different networks that can prove crucial in the search for fresh approaches.

(p. 65), Arnulf Keese (p. 93) and Xavier Randretsa (p. 194) for real live examples from management).

To give you an example, let's assume that the context mix in which you are embedded is dominated by network-like structures, say 70% as you have to align a global sales force. Let's further assume that you have to lead an employee, a local sales manager for example, for whom the network aspect is only marginal when it comes to time budgets or capacity for working in the network. You need to be aware that there is a danger in approaching the person with leadership initiatives that typically work best in the network context. Rather, use leadership approaches from family-like dominated contexts. The aim would then be to support the person in being more present in the network. This could be done by shaping their mental model of the network and its purpose as an extended version of their local family and creating a sense of belonging for the person to the global family of sales people. This also includes local stakeholder management, e.g. by involving the local management the person is reporting to.

However, in order to be able to do this we need a kind of "early warning system" or "default reflection process" in order to force you to check the complexity mix of the context of those you are dealing with and then compare it. To be a good leader, you should always know where you are coming from and what kind of filters are acting in your personal perception of the world and you should be able to step into the shoes of the others to try to see the world through their eyes.

In order to support you in the process we created a little visualization tool that "forces" you to think about the mix you are in e.g. by creating a little pie chart of your mix: family x%, machine y%, network z%.

Then step, for example, into the shoes of the employee (or business units or customers, etc.) you want to support and create the same pie chart from his or her hypothetical perspective (if possible check your hypotheses with the real perspective of the person).

Now compare these to pie charts and draw conclusions from the similarities and differences.

To make this comparison easier we have a different way to visualize the two context mixes that you would like to take into account. This goes as follows:

Visualize your context

Please draw a pie chart that shows the contextual mix in which your leadership task is embedded. Then, depending on the leadership initiative you plan to start, draw this mix as a concentric circle around the first "core". Use the same starting point. We typically use 12:00 as the starting mark.

Here is an example:

Figure 1.1: Complexity mix

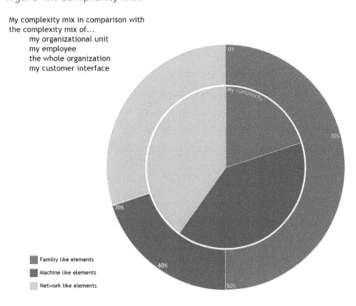

My complexity mix in comparison with the complexity mix of...
my organizational unit
my employee
the whole organization
my customer interface

Familiy like elements
Machine like elements
Network like elements

To come up with a rough estimate for the percentages of your personal mix you can either use your gut feeling which usually works great or you can use one or more of the leading questions which we have arranged in the triplets below. To answer them, think of your job description or your work schedule during a regular week.

1. To what degree do I have to attend to

- Personal relationships (or social presence; see chapter "Mastering technologies and creating online leadership identity", p. 122, and Part IV: Some concepts from "Closeness at a Distance", p. 296)? => % Family?

- Processes and their efficiency? => % Machine?

- The development and coordination of local or international networks? => % Network

2. I am mainly paid for

- Creating and maintaining a harmonious work climate => % Family

- Consolidating or optimizing processes => % Machine

- Increasing the organization's ability to innovate => % Network

3. In my work context, the type of closeness that is more critical is

- Personal closeness? => % Family

- Closeness to processes? =>% Machine

- Virtual closeness (see Part IV: Some concepts from "Closeness at a Distance", p. 296)? => % Network

4. My leadership task involves leading

- On a personal level => % Family

- According to key performance indicators for people and processes => % Machine

- Through influencing the environment and/or setting the right framework and allowing for self-organization => % Network

5. My leadership approach is best characterized by the

- Relationship a parent or an older friend has with a child => % Family

- Notion of a manager => % Machine

- Notion of a leader and/or a coach => % Network

6. Knowledge transfer or competence development in my context is most about

- Education and/or instruction => % Family

- Training => % Machine

- Self-organized and/or informal learning => % Network

You can apply these same questions also to assess the "outer ring" (employee, business unit, customer etc.), i.e. the complexity mix of your focus (e.g. your employees, your customers, etc.). Just replace "my" with "my customers", "my employees", etc.

Here is a template that you can use for your assessment:

Figure 1.2: Complexity mix template

My complexity mix in comparison with
the complexity mix of...
    my organizational unit
    my employee
    the whole organization
    my customer interface

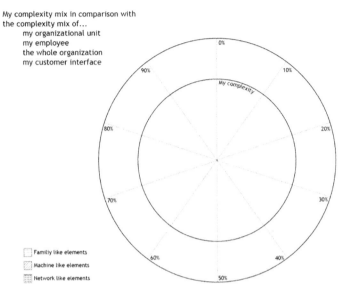

☐ Family like elements

▨ Machine like elements

▦ Network like elements

Part II: Dealing with your complexity mix

Introduction

Do you know what a paramecium is? In 2007, the paramecium was voted unicellular of the year, and in 2015 the German Society of Protozoology nominated it as the most attractive protozoan, an animal life form encompassing only one cell. The nomination was intended to make people aware of the importance of these life forms for our world's ecosystem.

Here is a sketch of a paramecium.

Figure 2.1: Paramecium

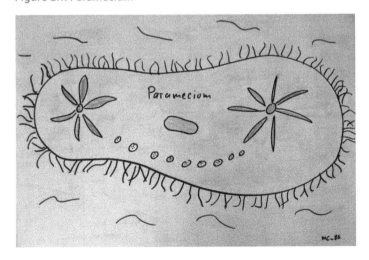

*We would like to take the praise even further by nominating this impressive animal as "Leader of the Year". Before we explain why, you may wonder why we chose a seemingly dumb animal to make a point about leadership. Clearly, we are not suggesting that the absence of intellect is a good prerequisite for being a successful leader. But we can learn a lot from the paramecium about the concepts of contextual intelligence and its application in contextual leadership (see chapter "Contextual leadership", p. 93), one of the six areas we will introduce in the following chapters.

The paramecium belongs to the unicellular species that has hundreds of cilia, little eyelash-shaped paddles around the cell. While it doesn't have significant brain capacity, it's still able to coordinate all those hundreds of paddles so it can move as a whole in a preferred direction. It does this very efficiently by manipulating its environment.

The environment wherein the animal is moving is denoted by hydrodynamic equations. These equations describe a kind of non-linear complexity that no man has ever been able to solve analytically. Also, there is no conductor sitting in the centre of the paramecium shouting "Row, row, row!" as it has no central brain to make all paddles row in the same direction at the same time.

Are you impressed? Can you do the same magic in your hyper-complex work environment?

What we are suggesting is this: As a network leader, you are asked to accomplish in a relatively short amount of time what nature has accomplished through evolution. That is creating, as part of setting the framework for your

---

* For a real life image of the paramecium see http://upload.wiki-media.org/wikipedia/commons/thumb/c/cb/Paramecium.jpg/220px-Paramecium.jpg.

team (see chapter "Mastering technologies and creating online leadership identity", p. 122) a system (an organizational unit) that is fully embedded in your organization and that is simultaneously

- separate from the organization to be able to pursue its own purpose or mission and move things into the direction of the leader's choice (see chapters "Navigating hyper-complexity", p. 39, and "Leadership branding", p. 65)

- connected to the organization in order to be part of the global information stream and influence it according to its needs (see chapters "Contextual leadership", p. 93, and "Shaping global dialogue", p. 159).

Based on this, your task is to attract a lot of people who will join your endeavours voluntarily and are ready to work together in one (possibly unknown) direction to mine the environment for new opportunities to thrive on.

First, this is about attractiveness. You as a leader with an authentic leadership brand (see chapter "Leadership branding", p. 65) should create

- as many followers as a paramecium has cilia and

- an attractive environment as well as a sense of belonging that provides your followers with a context wherein they are comfortable to live and work (see chapter "Contextual leadership", p. 93).

Second, it is about contextual intelligence and contextual leadership (see chapter "Contextual leadership", p. 93). This is where we can learn from our little one-cell star by understanding how it moves forward in its fluid habitat. So let's take a closer look.

Biophysicists in Juelich, Germany*, discovered in 2013 that the cilia (the eyelash shaped paddles of the paramecium) don't perform strokes synchronously like people in a rowing boat but rather create a movement similar to a self-organized 'la ola' wave performed by fans during sports events.

How does the paramecium achieve this and why is it more efficient than synchronous rowing?

According to current knowledge, there is no mastermind behind the movement that coordinates all those hundreds of little paddlers across space and time. Particularly, the paramecium doesn't analyze its complex environment before acting. It's the other way around instead.

Think of it like this:

1. There is a certain programme of movement all cilia share that is similar to swimming. You extend your arms before moving your hand backwards trying to create as much friction as possible before circling your arm back to its original position close to your body. [†]

2. In doing so, one of the cilia probes the surrounding fluid by stirring it up in a certain frequency and mode, thereby creating a little vortex-like current. So it acts and sees what happens as a result.

3. The fluid transports the little vortex to the neighbouring cilia of the same animal who can sense or are affected by it. If the vortex and the strength of the signals it sends fit whatever they are doing, they will start to do the same movements (with a little time lag!), thereby creating the same distortions in

---

* http://www.pnas.org/content/110/12/4470.abstract.

† This can be viewed as an analogy to the concept of the so-called non-negotiable behaviours, Herrero (2008).

the fluid, which, in turn, is then carried on to the next neighbours and so on and so forth.

4. Finally, the cilia that originated the movement will also be affected (again, with a certain time lag) by the current and the corresponding vortices created by the other cilia. Now, if the frequency and the mode of the vortex fit, the movement of the first cilia is reinforced and the whole cycle starts again, but now with a higher intensity and strength. Resonance has occurred and the whole system is moving in one direction on a wave that has been created by the paramecium itself. And riding on a wave is not only more fun than rowing synchronously, but even more efficient as the movement is completely in accordance with the non-linearity of the hydrodynamic equations. These equations belong to the most difficult ones in physics (and mathematics!) and so far, there is little knowledge on how they could be solved. They are supposed to describe the behaviour of liquids, especially water, even in turbulent conditions.

Nature can really stun us with its smart solutions! So what has all this to do with leadership in hyper-complex environments?

The answers are contained in the following main messages which also constitute the chapters in this part of the book.

<u>1. Navigating hyper-complexity</u> (p. 39)

Successful leadership always starts with leading yourself. You need to be immersed in your context in order to be able to deal with its hyper-complexity professionally. You also need to let go of the paradigm "think first and then act". And you need to be able to deal with the pressure caused by the complexity through self-management, just like the paramecium does. It balances the outside pressure of the fluid by ingesting part of it into its interior.

2. Leadership branding (p. 65)

Leaders without followers are just lonely nuts. What makes you attractive enough for others to follow you?

3. Contextual leadership (p. 93)

Having followers is not enough. You also have to keep them through motivation

4. Mastering technologies and creating online leadership identity (p. 122)

And by providing an attractive framework for collaboration

5. Shaping global dialogue (p. 159)

Networks consist only of individuals and their communication, which you actively need to shape to serve your purpose

6. Influencing the organization (p. 194)

In order to make individuals and teams successful, you also need to influence the respective organizational environments

Navigating hyper-complexity

Interview with Dr. Armin Klesing

Global Business Development Manager at Solvay Specialty Polymers

Figure 2.2: Armin Klesing's complexity image

Profile
- ❖ Global Business Development Manager at Solvay Specialty Polymers
- ❖ German
- ❖ 49 years old
- ❖ Married, two children
- ❖ Oversees on average 10 people worldwide

Dr. Armin Klesing has a PhD in chemical physics and a postgraduate degree in general management. He joined Solvay as a postdoc 20 years ago to work on computational design of advanced materials. However, driven by "the desire to find out how things work", after four years he went into sales, sales management, then marketing and business development to master the value chain of business on both ends. "My primary expertise lies at the interface of science and business. Taking my gut feel both as a technologist and a business person and trying to scope out what is doable at the edge of the possible … trying to do really new and different things."

Armin's interest is not so much in securing existing business. Rather, he feels that, "building new business from scratch is way more rewarding, both for yourself and the company, than managing existing business". He really likes to break new ground at the frontier of technology and science. His current mission is to "build Solvay's position in a changing aerospace industry".

Asked to describe himself, Armin answers, "I think I am strongly driven by the desire to increase my own complexity". He believes that on the philosophical level of personal development, "every person should strive to constantly increase his or her own complexity level". In doing so, "it is very important that you understand your own action logic. That you understand when you respond to a specific problem pattern in a specific way because you know it already. Or that you are aware of your own action logic if you approach a problem pattern that you do not recognize."

Armin values lifelong learning, measuring his personal learning curve by the degree of complexity and uncertainty a person can process. He applies this when observing others' learning processes. "Where are they on their life's complexity curve? Are they aware of their own action logic, their action patterns? Do they understand why they react in a certain way to certain problems, and where they are heading?"

With regard to his team, Armin stands for four things: transparency, fairness, trust and acting on clearly set expectations.

The complexity wherein Armin operates

"There are local ways of leading, local organizations, and local leadership concepts and requirements. And there are global requirements and global organizations." In consequence, Armin perceives two types of complexity. "One comes from the need to align local and global leadership. The other relates to global leadership that needs to hook up with a broad bandwidth of social and cultural backgrounds. When you act in an existing local business, it is more about dealing with the efficiency levels of people who are more or less culturally homogenous. In global business, however, the key thing is to manage the cultural diversity of people who have totally different backgrounds not only culturally but also socially and in terms of connectedness to their own historical past."

The bandwidth on a global level ranges from very low to very high social living standards and encompasses a variety of social organization and group dynamics. For example, Chinese managers whose parents were the losers of the Cultural Revolution are likely to have worked their way up from rather low social standards compared to the European or North American colleagues of the same generation. Because of this background, "they frequently have a strong desire to move up the social ladder quickly, and accordingly are ready to work for the level of success at the cost of loyalty to an employer", in Armin's experience. "Because of this great diversity of culturally, socially and historically conditioned motivations, leaders have to manage beyond efficiency and clarity of direction and alignment by acting as credible reference points and by developing trust across a broad bandwidth of cultural and social backgrounds."

When asked how much of Solvay is family, machine or network, he distinguishes between the organization as a whole and his own context.

Table 2.1: Armin Klesing's complexity mix

	The whole organization	Armin's specific job context
Network	20%	60%
Machine	60%	40%
Family	20%	0

Armin describes Solvay as a 152-year-old family organization. Compared to many other big corporations, Solvay is still partially family owned, and smaller production locations, rather than mega sites, as well as personal relationships are valued. On average, job satisfaction is quite high. This job satisfaction, says Armin, "also owes to the family factor which influences the way the network structure works. People want to belong to something and want to have the opportunity to create footprints in their own right."

Creating trust is related to this. "The whole point of a family organization is sustainable trust." The machine will only work if there is the same level of trust and respect everywhere because the processes and structures of the machine are built on that. Hence, "the machine factor of leadership forces you to put the same level of trust in people all over the planet wherever the organization is. We are no longer acting in the control mode of Manchester Capitalism."

This is a major challenge when considering cultural differences. While company loyalty is relatively high on average in the US, Japan and in many European countries, the workforce for example in China is more mobile. Staff fluctuate regularly towards better conditions. Therefore, the level of trust Western managers put in Chinese co-workers often tends to be lower compared to similarly bred Western colleagues. This, however, is not acceptable for Armin as trust over time triggers a concomitant, self-propelling collective action logic.

On average, Armin oversees ten employees who report to him full-time or part-time in regional sales organizations across the world. In the latter case, their relationships with Armin can be described as "dotted lines." Organizationally, they report to their local sales organization and functionally, they report to Armin. However, stresses Armin, "The number of direct reports is not really important in a global organization. What matters in a global organization is the impact factor. Do you lead for impact or not? I either have an impact on a person and a group of people or not. You have your own brand and it competes with other leadership brands. Based on their own ambitions and life-leadership stages the employees individually decide whom to follow within the boundaries of their assignments."

Armin's personal approach to leadership and creating followers comprises three central elements. First, "informal authority may be even more important than formal authority." This can be achieved through trust-based, informal lines of communication with the regional managers and people at all levels. Alignment results from a shared vision and overall objectives rather than inflexible execution. He grants his regional team members a reasonable level of autonomy for figuring things out their own way. According to Armin, this approach is known as mission command tactics in German military history.

Second, "If you want to lead in a global organization it must be clear that you put your own accountability first – you don't put your ego first. The leader is the root, the team members are the branches and the leaves. You want the customers to see the leaves, not the root. The root provides the water, the nutrition, but is not visible. It's not me who needs to shine. Rather, I'm accountable and responsible for making my people shine."

Third, Armin strives to lead through creating "visibility of performance and visible appreciation of performance." He works to motivate and activate his team members by expressing his appreciation (through an email message stating, "You did an excellent job", with everybody in cc, for example) or by inviting them to business fairs in Germany as appropriate.

Armin measures the impact of his leadership on two levels. On the machine level, success is measured through the number of needle-moving projects and their revenue potential. On the network level, the indicator is "the being well organized factor". Armin sees the latter as equally important because it functions as a process indicator or an early warning signal, whereas success on the machine level is an end-of-pipe indicator that hinges on the quality of a pre-defined process.

He measures "the being well organized factor" as follows. He visits his team members around the world twice a year on average and looks at how these visits are organized and executed locally. Is airport transfer organized? Who offers to pick him up in person? Are local people adjacent to the team informed about his visit and are they prepared to contribute to its success? How tight is the meeting schedule and is time used efficiently? How well are the customer and internal meetings prepared? etc. When, for example, customer meetings fail to yield the required results he knows he hasn't made sufficient impact on that specific local team. "When I don't make a needle-moving impact people rightfully feel that I am wasting their time. They will only follow me if they understand that through following me they can be successful professionally and make progress on their own life-leadership curve." Conversely, well-organized visits indicate that team members recognize the personal benefits of "following" Armin's leadership.

Armin's strategies to reduce and navigate this complexity: What has worked and what hasn't worked so well, and why?

"If I had to describe my responsibility, my job in a nutshell, I would say it is about trying to build a highway in the Amazonas, to build a highway in the jungle." Leadership matters most in the absence of structure. Everything becomes easy when there is a structure, even if it's a complicated one. To Armin, reducing complexity means building structure where there is none. "People understand that by building structure with you and for you they have the opportunity to shine themselves." In the absence of structure the risk of making mistakes is high. "Therefore you need to create an atmosphere of trust where people understand that they are allowed to make mistakes on their road to success, and they are committed to work hard to not disappoint." Mission command is the guiding principle.

Another strategy Armin uses to manage complexity is flexibility. "I lead by example, by giving clear directions and I do not ask anybody to put in working hours or travel commitments that I am not ready to demonstrate myself. I try to align people with my path. And it can be that after six months or one year of persistently forging a path we find that we need to change direction. And everyone who is on the team understands that he or she is encouraged to make an impact in this collective learning expedition."

Armin argues that it's not helpful to believe that there is only one valid path to which all must stick, no matter what. Rather, he strives to appreciate his people for their individual approaches for dealing with complexity and working out solutions that comply with a respective person's individual action logic.

"The leader completely owns the risk, he absorbs the risk, and the team owns the success. We have monthly 1-on-1 performance dialogues at the beginning or at the end of each month. We then discuss together the good, the bad and the ugly. After a month or two, we reevaluate: Did our assumptions match reality? If there are issues, can they be overcome by working on a person's self-awareness? etc."

Armin's reactions to the central parameters of leading in the face of hyper-complexity

- Shaping and influencing organizational communities – Yes. "People expect someone to be the leader, to give them direction that create meaning. It's very important that there are people who give that direction even if only informally."

- Creating virtual closeness and global collaboration spaces – Yes. "I call it the liquid organization. I actively encourage the team to not always work through me as the ring leader to globally create internal connections. If you have a problem and somebody else potentially has a piece of a solution, no matter where he is located, pick up the phone and give them a call. Make the other person proud to help you."

- Framework setting and mastering technology – Yes. Connect over media and build media competence. Most importantly, use video and telephone. Stop writing long emails that by definition are unidirectional and only make you sink deeper into your own beaten path.

- <u>Dealing with complexity</u> – Yes. In the absence of structure people can't know whether they are going to be successful. The leader has to mitigate the risk of people destroying, or fearing to destroy, themselves on the mission.

- <u>Personal branding</u> – Yes. At all times and especially in virtual environments leaders should be absolutely clear about their personal brand. The authentic and credible brand of the company and of the leaders is what attracts followers.

- <u>Contextual leadership</u> – Yes and no. While Armin agrees that context is key, he disagrees with the "customizing" element of contextual leadership. "The consistency of your action logic is what makes you credible. Your life philosophy, the way you want to achieve things is not something you can customize. We have our strengths and weaknesses. Leaders should enable people to become as complete as individuals as possible. The concept of customizing oneself is directly opposed to the concept of completeness. Having a personal brand means trying to be as complete as possible as a person, and this notion of completeness varies significantly across cultures. It's more about aligning people to an objective and for this, you have to be credible. Leadership is not so much about allowing people to self-organize as it is about thinking processes from their potential end point and establishing a mechanism for getting there much faster than things would flow on their own. As a leader you are the attractor in the system, the unifying flag in the ground, and you allow the people to decide by themselves what they want to be attracted to. It is the following that creates the leader."

- <u>Creating a culture of voicing and feedback</u> – Yes. "We base our after-action reviews on asking, what would we do if our lives depended on the way we execute, not just our money? This leads to more rigorous feedback on any mistakes made on the individual or organizational level. This approach helps to make people understand that feedback is not about criticism to make some people look bad but about figuring out how we can do things better collectively by putting aside egos. We play in the champions' league, not in the third league. At that level, being very good is not good enough."

- <u>Measuring success</u> – Yes. "I measure success by the being-well-organized factor. Beyond that, as in any company, success is, above anything else, financial success."

Navigating hyper-complexity: Personal reflection

Imagine finding yourself thrown into a context you have never before experienced with such intensity. You didn't volunteer for this; rather, things just turned out this way. And you happen to be accountable for navigating this context successfully. Does this scenario sound familiar to you? If so, have you

- felt that you are in control of it all?

- felt powerless and swept along like a leaf in the wind?

- felt that somehow you can muddle your way through this complexity?

What is your attitude when dealing with complex and unfamiliar situations?

Having the appropriate attitude when encountering unfamiliar situations is the first step toward dealing with them professionally. If the circumstances seem to make you powerless, you can turn to professional self-management and expectation management to empower yourself. On the other hand, feeling in control of a situation when really you are not can lead to severe mistakes.

Take a moment to reflect on your approach to dealing with dilemmas. What is your attitude? Do you recognize any of the above? Do you feel in control, do you feel powerless, or do you muddle your way through?

Armin Klesing is a good example of a leader who understands and appreciates complexity, both individual complexity and organizational complexity arising from cultural differences and the interplay between local and global business structures. Armin knows that leadership's responsibility is not to fight complexity or work against it but rather, to work with it and understand its importance. He understands that this is best done by offering a flexible structure where there is none. The balance between building structure and maintaining flexibility as well as mirroring and challenging his people to reach their best constitute Armin's unique leadership brand.

Problem solving and decision-making, besides people management, are two of the most significant tasks of a manager. There are different approaches to mastering them. Knowing which approach to use in the appropriate context is a critical prerequisite to effective problem-solving and decision-making, and hence to structuring and reducing hyper-complexity. In this chapter, we will show you how.

Leadership approaches to problem solving and decision-making

Classification of situation types

We use the following two dimensions to structure contexts, and the corresponding approaches to problem solving.

- How precise and complete is your understanding of the present state of the system (i.e. the context) you are dealing with? Asked differently, how predictable are the current state and future development of this system?

- How many different elements and factors describe the context wherein the situation is embedded?

Using these two dimensions we can classify the different types of situations:

Figure 2.3: Classification of situations

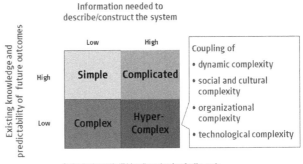

Further development by Hildebrandt 2014, based on: Camillus. 2008; Snowden & Boone. 2007; Mason & Mitroff. 1981

Classification of situations: 4 types

We have identified four groups of situations that we come across in our daily work.

Simple situations

Simple situations
- You have complete knowledge of the current state and all possible future states of the system;
- There is only one, or a few, variables at most and you have complete control over them;
- You know exactly what you want to achieve.

Unique and optimal solutions exist for this type of situation. It is only a matter of mathematics/economics to figure the solution out and base one's decision on it. This is the realm of "best practice" and "benchmarks".

Complicated situations

Complicated situations
- The number of variables you have to control is higher;

- In most cases the solution or decision has to be compatible with different, sometimes even conflicting quality criteria or goals.

This is the realm of "good practice", optimal control theory and stakeholder management to identify priorities.

Complex situations

Complex situations

- The number of variables that shape the system is small; there is only one dynamic pattern ("attractor") describing the overall dynamics of the system;

- The understanding of the present situation and future development is weak.

As it's impossible to make ex-ante predictions about the development of this system, the notions of solution and good practice break down for this group of situations. Instead, the navigator will try to identify the underlying dynamic pattern and the corresponding control variables that shape this system, using this knowledge to influence the system towards reaching a stable and stationary state.

A well-known example for a control variable is coming directly from our kitchen. Just by increasing or decreasing the temperature of a pot filled with water a system can be changed from a chaotic state into a state of superior order where hexagonal convection cells are formed.

Figure 2.4: Water surface*

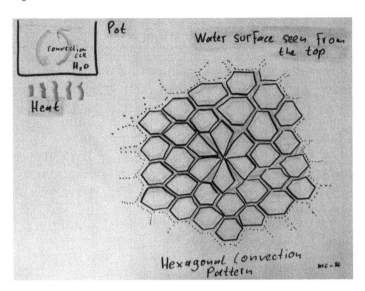

A subset of these complex situations is constituted by so-called deterministic chaotic systems and fractals with their richness of visible structures that can be constructed using a source code of few bits.

Could there also be a single control variable that changes societies from chaotic to ordered states? We will leave the answer and its possible implications to the reader's musings.

Hyper-complex situations

Hyper-complex situations

- The number of variables that shape this system is large. Several dynamic patterns ("attractors") from different sources of complexity are present here and linked with each other;

- The understanding of the present situation and future development is weak.

---

* For a real picture see http://www.uni-graz.at/~huber/ahlectures/ content/lecture01/img/energyInput_waterSurface.jpg.

So far, mathematics and physics have little to no knowledge that would enable us to deal with hyper-complex systems systematically. Hence we have to break new ground, which is why we include in this book interviews with leaders and managers about their perspectives and experiences with hyper-complex environments (see also the introductory interviews in each chapter and Part III of the book). We asked them to describe the complexity wherein they operate and how they deal with it. Find below some hints compiled from the interviews.

While all four types of situations exist in all organizations, we are most interested in complex and hyper-complex situations in this book. So let´s take a closer look at them.

You can recognize a complex situation when these two statements apply:

Complex
situations

- It's no longer possible to describe the current state of the system precisely; and

- The elements – in most cases individuals but also whole organizational units – that constitute the system form an interacting network that can self-organize. Understanding such a system is a bit like predicting next year's weather: virtually impossible.

In this context, controlling/predicting/ steering/ picking a solution/ determining have another, more dynamic meaning as we know from the butterfly effect. And certain concepts such as average behaviour tend to be meaningless. Instead, social networks are about attractors, hubs and weak links.

An attractor is something that pulls people or the elements of a system towards them, thereby forming major hubs in the network. Good examples are people or platforms like Google, YouTube, Facebook or WhatsApp that create large numbers of followers (see Part IV: "The concepts of

Attractors

groups, networks and communities, p. 269, for further information on this).

Here we distinguish between two different situations:

- Unpredictable systems with only one attractor (e.g. dictatorships). If the boundary conditions can be changed to create one stable attractor the system will be aligned completely. Found on the darker side of society and power, this phenomenon is known as the "slaving principle" in physics. Adolf Hitler, through his communication campaign implemented by Joseph Goebbels, succeeded in creating one attractor (fascism) within society and thereby complete alignment of the majority of the population.

- Systems that may have more than one attractor (e.g. systems with different political parties; organizations with diverse leadership and attractive personal branding (see chapter "Leadership branding", p. 65) etc.). Members of such systems are constantly pulled from one attractor to another (social complexity). They oscillate, show erratic behaviour (dynamic complexity), pattern formation (emerging complexity) and never really reach a stable and static state. These systems are always in a "critical" state.

Allow us a quick observation about human behaviour. We can never really know what is going on inside other people. Often we don't even have enough conscious knowledge about ourselves. And we can never really know what state our communication partner is in. People behave in complex and unpredictable ways. On the other hand, people may also choose to behave in a deterministic way: If I give you this then you will do that. People in high managerial positions may tend to perceive the organization as a deterministic system that can be steered by cause and effect (power and control). At the same time, people on a lower hierarchical level may experience the same organization as complex and unpredictable and feel powerless when they are asked to steer. Both perceptions can be right.

Experience suggests that success depends on the ability to adopt different approaches in the respective contexts.

Figure 2.5: Different situations require different behaviour

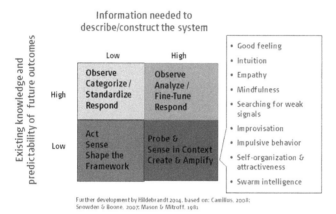

We recommend applying different strategies to the different situations. Here are some examples.

Different strategies for different situations

Simple situations

Observe the typical failures in a production process, categorize them using, for example, an Ishikawa Diagram[*] and aim for a zero failure approach. If you have to insert a green and a red light bulb to a product and you know that the positions are sometimes reversed in the assembly process then think of means that make it impossible to insert the red light bulb to the socket of the green one and vice versa (e.g. by having different sockets for the different bulbs).

---

[*]   Ishikawa (1990).

Complicated situations

Observe the performance of different products in different markets. Analyze your product portfolio and its implementation for conflicting goals and processes concerning the organizational strategy. Set new strategic rules to get better results from your overall portfolio, e.g. by giving up "local" success patterns in favour of better global performance.

Complex situations

This should be the realm of Change Management: you have a clear idea about what has to be changed and start a large-scale to achieve that goal. You are perceptive to human reactions to the initiative, both the positive and the negative ones. Based on that knowledge you shape your approach so that positive behaviour is amplified and problems are resolved.

Hyper-complex situations

In the following, we will focus on strategies for hyper-complex situations and the second type of systems described above: those with multiple attractors and the corresponding problems and approaches to solving them.

Here is a short exercise designed to help you train this ability by looking into the recent past to analyze your own professional context.

- Try to identify at least one example from your work experience for each of the situations discussed above: simple situation, complicated situation, complex situation, hyper-complex situation.

- How did you respond to the different problems? What were your experiences? What worked and why? What didn't work and why not?

How to deal with hyper-complexity

A good starting point for improving your professional competence to deal with hyper-complexity is learning to use all the inner resources human beings dispose of. The image below illustrates those resources.

Inner resources

Figure 2.6: Intelligence, wisdom, creativity, affect

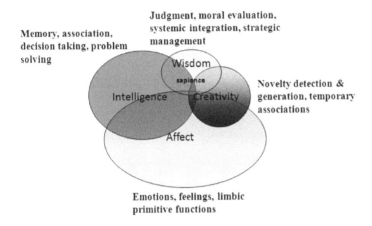

Graphic from http://faculty.washington.edu/gmobus/TheoryOf Sapience/SapienceExplained/1.sapienceintroduction/sapiencein-troduction_files/mindConstructs.png

We'd like to highlight the two facts that are important for us here.

1. All of the three brain functions of intelligence, creativity and wisdom are linked with affect. Drawing on affect for complex problem solving is therefore critical.

2. In their relation to affect, creativity, wisdom and intelligence can be considered to a certain extent as different ways of processing the world. This is why it's beneficial to know the strengths and weaknesses of these different ways of dealing with our complex world and act accordingly.

The graphic also suggests how everyday language could be mapped to human inner resources. Intuition could be linked to creativity; the gut feeling may relate to affect; and the experience of something feeling right (total conviction/rules of thumb/heuristics) could be associated with wisdom. Different cultures call these ways of processing information differently. For example, the role and description of emotions varies significantly across the world. If this applies to your culture, how would you re-label the areas shown in the graphic? Also, rational reasoning/rational problem solving that is often perceived to not take emotions into account may be associated with that part of intelligence that doesn't overlap significantly with affect.

Intuition and gut feeling

We would like to suggest that intuition and gut feeling are in fact two separate resources and can therefore be cultivated in different ways. While the gut feeling is based on careful observation of body signals and the corresponding emotions in decision-making processes, intuition is connected with our internal source of creativity and wisdom[*]. We believe that managers who know how to draw from both and harness the respective hints from their unconscious in their decision-making tend to make better decisions.

Dealing with the unknown

Coming back to our hyper-complex environments, the competence of dealing with the unknown is crucial. It consists of two basis elements:

1. Sufficient psychic ability to endure, and even accept, the state of not knowing without giving in to the urge to act.

---

[*] See a short essay by Baltzer and Hildebrandt (see Part IV: "Identifying and applying our inner resources to complex decision-making", p. 281) for more information on inner resources and their role in individual decision-making processes, including practical methods.

2. The ability to use information from our senses when dealing with contexts that are either characterized by too much information or by scarcity of relevant data.

Consider the following scenario to better understand the psychological dimension of this.

While travelling, you have an unexpected stopover in a large airport where all signs are in a language unfamiliar to you. Information in English is nowhere to be found. You are entirely lost and time is running. This is a complex situation. While some people might panic and jump to action by following the crowd, others may become angry or frustrated and complain about the absence of guidance for international travellers. Still others might despair and cry, thinking they will never find their way. Yet another reaction could be asking a random person for directions, risking being misled. Or one might freeze and beat oneself up for "always ending up in situations like this", spinning into a downward spiral by imagining the worst possible outcome.

All of these reactions are based on the expectation that a readily available programme will guide one through the situation. The brain will conjure up action that is informed by past experience, assuming that this would provide a solution. Ask people and you will get the right answer; follow the crowd and you will get to the right place; use the information system to guide you; communicate to others your helplessness and they will take responsibility and guide you out.

However, if you stood still and observed your environment and your own reaction for a moment, you would likely begin to perceive patterns. You may realize that there are several streams of people. You may be able to distinguish people who are arriving from those who are departing through subtle differences in their facial expressions, by seeing more people dressed in local attire (domestic versus international flights), by the appearance of their luggage (in good condition or torn and dirty; with or without tags). The longer you wait and observe, the higher the chance that you will finally walk in the right direction. Of course, you will double-check and continue to observe on the way.

This example shows how our brains are programmed to deal with problems and that we tend to act for action's sake when overwhelmed with complexity. Perceived pressure from the environment leads to the assumption of being expected to demonstrate leadership by taking decisions and acting swiftly. This, however, is only a successful strategy for simple or complicated problems.

Sensing, probing and analyzing while being immersed in the context

In hyper-complexity, discerning patterns that will point to solutions requires immersion in the context. It can't be achieved by stepping out of the situation or context and thinking about it only then. Rather, one needs to sense and respond to the situation in the moment of its happening, while observing: How is the system reacting to my response? Is it moving towards or away from my response? Are (small) adjustments or fine-tuning necessary before moving on?

Sensing, probing and analyzing are activities that almost need to take place simultaneously when starting a leadership initiative in a hyper-complex context.

So we are well advised to learn to create and maintain an inner state that is a bit like a sponge. We observe and sense, suspending immediate judgment and jumping to conclusions, absorbing all available information until we are fully immersed with all our senses. This information-gathering phase is not guided by rational thinking as thinking often leads to filtering through judgment and prioritization. Rational approaches are characterized by the paradigm of focusing on the essential. This, however, prevents us from discovering the new and the innovative. The advent of new ideas and innovation is accompanied usually only by weak signals. Consider the following metaphor.

When searching the night sky for a particular faint star, it often vanishes when you focus your eyes on it. This is because when we focus on an object, the light falls on those areas of our retina where receptors specialize in dealing with high-intensity light. However, when slightly blurring the focus, the star becomes visible because the light now falls on those areas of the eye that process and amplify weak intensities.

Just like taking out the intense focus in the star gazing metaphor, we need to wait, observe and feel with all our senses and retain an open state of mind. We should keep this open and slightly blurry state of mind until we become aware of weak signals or stronger patterns and sense: Yes, this could be it. This is the starting point for probing, the next step in the sensing-probing-analyzing sequence.

However, allow us to clarify an important misconception. We don't propose a new rationalist model in the tradition of "first think then act" to pre-analyze a situation before even planning to act by taking even more parameters into account. Rather, think of leaders in hyper-complexity as jazz musicians who improvise. They sense and simultaneously process the parameters that constitute their context while being immersed in a situation or interaction with team members and partners, acting according to what they think and feel is the right thing to do in that particular moment (see chapter "Contextual leadership", p. 93).

Probe and sense, create and amplify

Probe and sense, create and amplify:

- Do you receive positive resonance from the system? For example, are people moving towards you to join you in your initiative or are they moving away from you, ignoring your initiative or even resisting?

- How can you amplify this positive resonance?

- Can you become yourself a new attractor in the system when pursuing this avenue?

Let's now look at the following questions:

- What is actually happening when patterns or weak signals appear to show us ways to deal with the complexity?

- Where does the strong feeling or conviction that we should pursue this approach and not another come from?

Intuition

We believe that being deeply convinced of doing the "right" thing is critical for successful leadership. If you are convinced, your body language and the words you say tend to match. People who listen to you can often feel that. You are in what others may perceive as an authentic state of mind. Thus your arguments can be more convincing and people tend to believe in you and follow you (see chapter "Leadership branding", p. 65). This, in turn, may increase the likelihood of implementing your leadership initiative successfully, reinforcing the conviction of doing the right thing.

Of course this comes with a caveat. Human conviction of doing the right thing is always just one side of the story that may not be shared by others. Therefore you need to scan your environment for positive resonance to what you believe in.

On the other hand, if resonance to your ideas or actions is negative, even just slightly so, know that you don't have to rely solely on rational conviction and gut feeling. To explain this, assume the following. You think that something has to be changed in your organization. You can prove the need for this change and your gut feeling tells you that you are right. Some people in your environment even have positive reactions to your idea. Still, nothing happens, things don't seem to move. Then one morning you wake up and your intuition tells you clearly not to push the idea any further. Your unconscious, through being immersed in the organizational context daily and processing the corresponding information, has understood that the organization is not ready for the change. You can then either continue to fight or listen to your inner wisdom and let it go. Perhaps another opportunity will come in the future.

When you don't take your intuitive, unconscious wisdom seriously, you may make a poor decision and fail. And just like the paramecium shows (see p. 33), you won't receive the necessary cues from your unconscious when you aren't an integral and active part of the system wherein you operate.

You can also think of an idea that doesn't fly in terms of bubbles in a glass of soda. Bubbles rise to the surface at different speed levels. Some rise immediately and fast, others rise later and slower. Rather than obsessing with the bubbles that don't rise immediately, we suggest focusing your energy on the ones that rush, trusting that bubbles will rise when the time is right.

In the interview with Arnulf Keese (p. 93), Arnulf encapsulates this principle when he explains his credo of "Reject, reject, commit". Be prepared to fight for what you believe in but know when to let go and go with the flow.

"Reject, reject, commit"

Drawing on inner resources can be challenging in our high-paced daily lives. Mindfulness practice is one useful way of training our minds to become conscious and aware of the relevant signals from the unconscious. Another useful self-development tool is the Personal Leadership practice developed by Barbara F. Schaetti et al., particularly the Critical Dialogue Method[*].

Exercise

How well do you use your intuition? Do you tap into this source when at work? Do you value it as much as your cognitive faculties?

1. Over the next few days, try to observe yourself. What feels "right" to you but isn't being realized? When and how do you know that it's time to let go?

2. Think of situations when your gut feeling told you that something was not right. Try to identify the signals you felt in your body. How and where do they manifest themselves?

Summary

It is important to know which kind of problem you are facing. Different problems need different approaches to solve them. Knowing how to access and use inner resources is key for problem-solving and successful leadership. Gut feeling and intuition are particularly crucial resources. In order to use them wisely, a person must be truly immersed in their organizational context for signals from the unconscious mind arise best in the thick of the relevant context. The trick is to stay open and allow information to flood you and enwrap you. You don't need to know right away what to do with it. There is no need to find the "right" solution immediately. Just remain conscious, aware and open to receive the signals that will point you in the best direction.

---

[*]   Schaetti et al. (2008).

Leadership in hyper-complex environments

In order to be a powerful and attractive magnet, leaders need to understand and communicate two central messages:

1. Who am I as a leader? What are my value propositions? What makes me attractive for the organization and possible followers? à personal leadership branding and

2. How do I retain, motivate and lead followers? à contextual leadership

In the following we take a closer look at personal leadership branding (p. 65) and, subsequently, at contextual leadership (p. 93). Together, these two chapters present two of the main personal levers concerning leadership in hyper-complex environments.

Leadership branding

Interview with Dr. Christian Ecke

Senior Director of Global Billing and Payments at eBay International AG

Figure 2.7: Christian Ecke's complexity image

Profile

❖ Senior Director of Global Billing and Payments at eBay International AG
❖ German
❖ 43 years old
❖ Married, two children
❖ Oversees 130 people worldwide

We (Line Jehle and Dr. Christian Ecke who have known each other for many years) had agreed to conduct a video interview using Skype. When the video functionality initially failed, Christian swiftly transferred our meeting to an alternative video solution and set up the call within minutes. Being a successful and experienced global leader, he knows that video is critical in virtual communication to create a personalized atmosphere, and he didn't want to proceed with the interview without the visual component. His technical competence is matched by his presence throughout our communication. He actively engaged with the webcam and listened intently. He is a communicator.

As a leader at eBay, Christian has constantly taken on more responsibility leading global teams in Europe, the US and Asia. When he is not travelling, a large part of his workday is virtual since he works from his home office. In order to be close to his family, he converted his garden house into an office from where he leads and manages a team of 130 people who are dispersed across the globe.

The complexity wherein Christian operates

Christian's team members come from many different cultural backgrounds. Most of them are young and highly media and tech literate.

As Senior Director of Global Billing and Payments, the topics he works on always have a global and a regional angle because global payment systems need to be adapted to the respective regions.

When Christian is not travelling and working from a regional office or with a peer team, he is physically disconnected because he works from his home office. However, he effectively connects with his peers and team members virtually.

He rates the organizational context he works within as 70% network, 25% machine, and 5% family. Overall, he describes the structure as a hybrid with characteristics of all the above.

While he describes the network and matrix structures as very efficient, communication poses a great challenge in both structures in his opinion, especially in the virtual space. Because the concept of organizing (whether in the machine or in the network) also means categorizing. "But can we still afford to categorize in our interconnected working world?" Christian asks. "Working has become so complex it even defies clear descriptions of functions or classification in organizational categories. Cross-functional teams, by their very nature, transcend categories and functions. This is what makes them potentially so successful," states Christian.

He adds that in the network it can be difficult to find the responsible and/or "right" decision-makers. Christian works to maintain clear structures within his team and also recognizes that the team forms part of the whole network where many different teams and decision-makers work on any one project. And because projects are no longer managed top-down, different functional areas overlap and merge, leading to inter-dependencies. It is complex.

Christian's strategies to reduce and navigate this complexity: What has worked and what hasn't worked so well, and why?

Christian continues, "The problem with networks is it's relatively easy to deny responsibility. If an issue isn't resolved immediately, it likely won't be resolved several months down the line." He believes to avoid hiding behind the network requires persistence. He won't leave a meeting before a result is reached. Traditional hierarchy may be absent, but tasks have to be fulfilled nonetheless. It's the leader's responsibility to guide the team and make decisions as well as activate the network and bring people together. This requires sound and constant moderating skills – something Christian demonstrates efficiently and convincingly during our conversation.

When comparing the virtual to the local realm, Christian sees the greatest difference between the two spheres in terms of intimacy and physical nearness. "Connecting on an emotional level is essential in the network. Colleagues tend to share much more private and business information when we're together physically." When working together in the same physical space, problems tend to be solved over a cup of coffee, and information can be obtained more easily. Global cooperation requires more organizing and structuring of elements such as time zones, technology or fixed meeting times, which necessitates a greater effort. Working together at a distance is more complex than working together locally and can sometimes feel unreal. In a physically shared office, one becomes aware of tensions and problems quickly and can react fast as part of a natural ongoing communicative process. In a remote environment, this is very difficult if not impossible due to the absence of this natural communication.

It is therefore absolutely necessary to show one's leadership brand online, Christian believes. "Don't confuse personal branding with self-marketing. What's important is that your people know you and understand what you are like, how you think and act and why. If you don't show this clearly, a wrong image of you may spread quickly in networks. Take an example: There are these two people I met only once, and in the brief interactions, I made just a few statements. Afterwards I learned that they judged me entirely based on this one encounter and the few comments I made. What I took away from this is that I need to be even more self-aware on how I share opinions and information with people I do not interact with frequently compared to working closely with people in one location."

To simulate local reality and master these challenges, Christian has established open chat forums within his team to foster an informal exchange on a voluntary basis.

He describes the virtual communication dilemma like this: 50% of his team members are content with increased communication and have a desire for even more. The other half prefer to communicate less in favour of getting their work done.

Christian believes that emotional connections are paramount in the network. It is therefore important to meet in person from time to time and to maintain a regular communication rhythm in the meantime.

Christian's reactions to the central parameters of leading in the face of hyper-complexity

• Shaping and influencing organizational communities – Yes

• Creating virtual closeness and collaboration spaces – Yes

• Framework setting and mastering technology – Yes

• Dealing with complexity – Yes

• Personal branding – Yes, very important!

• Contextual leadership -Yes

• Creating a culture of voicing and feedback – Yes. Feedback is given much more frequently face-to-face. This must be compensated in the virtual realm.

• Measuring success – Yes. Make your successes really visible! Personalize them and celebrate them openly.

Leadership branding

One of us (Line Jehle) recently gave a speech at a major tech company about global leadership. One of the central statements strongly echoed by the audience was that in complex global organizations, it is the followers who decide what constitutes a good leader or manager.

Think about the leaders you have worked with. Whom would you happily follow and support, and why? Conversely, are there managers you are glad not to be working with any longer? And why?

Now try to define your personal brand as a leader – the bundle of unique characteristics, attitudes and values that you stand for and that make you attractive within the organization. Can you describe your leadership brand?

In this chapter, we will grapple with the leadership phenomenon of personal branding: of how the network leader can make herself visible, recognizable and attractive in an authentic way.

Christian Ecke is a good example of a leader who is very present in online meetings. He is able to transport his personality and leadership identity virtually. After talking to him, you have a clear picture of the person and what it would be like to work with him. You feel that he "sees" you. He wants the video to be on, he wants to see how you react to the conversation and he is ready to share some of his privacy with you online. After an online meeting with Christian you feel that you just had a real encounter. In short, Christian has a clear leadership branding, including you in what is happening right now locally and globally, practicing contextual leadership.

This chapter will take a closer look at personal leadership branding, while the subsequent chapter will deal with contextual leadership.

Followers decide what constitutes good leadership

What is your personal leadership brand?

Why is personal branding becoming more important in network organizations?

Good leadership is determined by different factors in the family, the machine and the network

Traditionally, the task of managers and leaders, particularly in matrix organizations, was to serve the organizational system by fulfilling certain roles and the corresponding tasks. In global network environments, and particularly in the virtual world, leadership and followership obey very different principles compared to local environments. Due to complexity and geographical distance, power structures and dynamics change. While in family and machine like organizational contexts the parameters that constitute good leadership are set by the organization through functional structures, processes and a clear hierarchy, this is different in the network. In network contexts, it's the leader's task to pull followers toward her by creating a transparent and attractive work environment. It is her task to display to her followers the benefits of following her so that they are empowered to choose.

In the network, it's no longer about what you say but about the response you get

What constitutes good leadership is now determined more by the quality of the followers and to a lesser degree by the leader. From a communications perspective, it is not about what you say but about the response you get.

From the industrial age to the knowledge era to the era of ideas, control loses significance

With an economy that has evolved from the industrial age to the knowledge era, and most recently to the era of ideas, creativity and innovation drive leadership more than ever before in modern history. Ideas can't be controlled or captivated in the same way we attempted to control and captivate knowledge. Ideas are the stuff from which the entrepreneurial spirit is made that is so characteristic of network organizations. Leadership must create the kind of fertile ground needed to attract people who create ideas.

In order to understand the concept of the follower who is drawn by the leader's attractiveness, think of it like this. Every employee of an organization has a limited amount of resources in terms of time and energy. A certain amount of those resources is needed for the local team context. They are the employee's duties, the non-negotiable part of the work. Now, the network side of the organization demands its employees to invest another part of their resources in global projects and activities. These activities are manly delivered without clear structure, roles and responsibilities and may therefore be perceived as riskier. The employee therefore needs to decide how to spread and invest his resources wisely. The possible impact of this decision on his career will play an important role in this. A follower is therefore someone who has made a conscious decision to invest a certain amount of his resources in the global network or community. Such investment is utterly needed in any matrix organization to fulfil its purpose, but cannot be forced sustainably in any way. We call these resources the corporate volunteering resources.

Followership flows from a leader's attractiveness

The more people a leader attracts, the more his attractiveness increases and he begins to act as a hub in the network or community. This enables him to influence the network or community significantly – an essential prerequisite to shaping and steering parts of the organization on a higher level.

Remember the self-organization phenomena of the "paddles" of our famous paramecium (p. 33). Do the leader and her leadership initiative make the right paddle stroke in order to start a movement that others will follow in a self-organized way? If so, the organization is able to move in the desired direction.

In many ways, network-like organizations are market places, arenas where stakeholders fight for corporate volunteering resources. Because the network organization with its focus on people's purpose and identity, rather than their tasks and roles, demands that its people decide how to distribute their time and energy most efficiently to best serve the organization's and their own needs. Essentially, the question is: Which leader do I follow?

Three central questions guiding leadership in the network

According to the principle of attractiveness, leadership in network environments is therefore guided by three central questions:

- How do I attract the right people (resources) for my purpose?

- Do they like working for me?

- Does following me make sense for them?

If the answer to the last question is No, people are likely to continue putting all their effort into their local teams and tasks instead of the global network projects and will feel torn between the two (and often more than two) at the same time. This is why working in the network needs to be attractive. It is the leader's task to make sure it is. Personal leadership branding makes an important contribution to achieving this.

Defining personal leadership branding

Our "leadership as a restaurant" metaphor

Think of leadership as a restaurant for a moment. A restaurant has an outside and an inside. Its appearance – the menu and the interior design that can be seen from the outside – determines how it's perceived by passers-by. If people decide to enter the restaurant, which also depends on whether they are hungry or not, the service, the quality of the food and the overall degree of expectations met will determine whether the guest is satisfied and likely to come back. Guest behaviour plays a role in this also. If a guest disturbs other guests he may be asked to leave and not come back.

The same principles apply to leadership. The leader's appearance attracts followers – or not. Those who decide to follow the leader will be exposed to the inside world of her leadership. The quality of the experience, the follower's motivation and the degree of matching expectations determine whether he is invited to stay and actually decides to do so.

Hence in order to attract followers, leaders need to make sure that

How do leaders attract followers?

- their outside leadership appearance matches the experience people make when getting to know the inside aspects of their leadership approach;

- they attract the right people instead of those who aren't a good fit for the work; and

- followers want to stay.

That's the leader's brand. It's what she stands for, what working with her is like, the initiatives/topics she is working on, what her leadership style is like, etc. It's her architecture and interior design and depending on an individual's taste, he may be drawn to that. Or he decides to follow a different leader whose look and feel is more appealing to him.

Crucially, leadership branding is not about being everybody's darling or trying to be appealing to everyone. It also isn't something that can be reinvented arbitrarily as it's intimately connected to one's biography, core values and personality.

Going back to the restaurant metaphor, here are some more similarities to take into account. A restaurant owner wants his place to prosper and not only attract passersby but find regular customers. Conversely, the customer's decision to stay at the restaurant and come back regularly as well as recommend it to others co-determines the place's success. In addition to an aesthetically pleasing environment and good food – characteristics fulfilled by many restaurants – customers will most likely recommend a restaurant because their very own expectations are met and because they are recognized and valued as individuals.

Will working with a particular leader further a potential follower's career?

Therefore many people will check before following a leader whether working with that particular person and group will benefit their own success story. Because if that is unlikely, why waste precious lifetime?

In her interview, Patricia Anthony (p. 245) sums up what working with her is like when she says, "People would say that I am very direct. I do not like to leave anything up to interpretation. Some people do say I have patience, but I am often seen as somebody who really pushes things. So do my staff have patience with me? I think, yes, in some ways. I think that they see me as a team player and somebody who will stand up for them, someone who's interested in their growth. I think one of the biggest problems in the world we have today is that we have too many people with big egos asking, 'what is in it for me?' and I do not believe in that philosophy. If somebody in my team can do something better than me I would like to promote them for it. Maybe they can teach me and I think that in the long run, we are going to get somewhere better. So I believe a leader's job is to grow their people and to give them the best opportunities and I think as an outcome overall business or operation will do better. So I am a very, very big proponent of true teamwork, it is more important than what is in it for me."

Virtual Closeness

Another key success factor for a good leader-follower match is the perception of virtual closeness[*] (see Part IV: "Some concepts from 'Closeness at a Distance'", p. 296).

---

[*] Hildebrandt et al. (2013), chapter 1.

The "inside of the restaurant" is where people come to work with the leader. In order to motivate people to enter, feel comfortable and inspired to stay and make it "the place to be", the leader needs to make sure that people have what they need to perform on the highest possible level. How is this best done? In terms of our metaphor, by decorating and filling the restaurant, the space of inter-action, with relevant objects, clear procedures, routines and guidelines, productive and attractive methods, supportive technology, human and professional encoun-ters, inspiring and challenging projects, etc. Through this, the leader performs the central task of framework setting (see chapter "Mastering technologies and creating online leadership identity", p. 122). In part, this is a collabora-tive endeavour. While some elements are set solely by the leader, others are co-created by the leader and the followers. Together, they design and build the inside of their workplace to create a sense of belonging* (see Part IV: "Some concepts from 'Closeness at a Distance'", p. 296).

However, leaders don't live in isolated spaces. They are embedded in organizational contexts. Consider this example: Munich, the capital of Bavaria, has strict building regulations to ensure architectural harmony across the city. Other parts of Germany, for example Berlin, see less regulation and an ensuing larger degree of architectural diversity.

Applied to our topic, if an organization is rather rule-oriented like Bavaria, it will require its leaders to adhere to a certain overall image. On the contrary, if an organi-zation is more like Berlin, its mix of people is likely more colourful and diverse, allowing different leadership approaches to coexist.

---

*   Ibid.

Assessing the leader-follower match

Either way, the purpose a leader pursues must be aligned with the organization's goals and strategy.

In summary, a leader is attractive for his followers when they can answer yes to questions like:

- Can I grow while working with you and your team and on your topics?

- Can I gain visibility and influence within the organization when working with you?

- Do you absorb the risk of failure when we try to break new ground?

- Do you share my (professional) values and worldview? If not, they may be so interesting, though, that I might still want to become involved and personally grow in this.

This approach to leadership suggests a significant change in leaders' perspectives. Rather than needing to be attractive in the eyes of their managers, leaders in complex global environments need to be attractive in the eyes of the people who work with them. It is indeed the war for talents in the global economy.

Creating your personal leadership brand: Things to consider from the beginning

Who and who not?

The most important thing a leader needs to find out is who he does and does not want to attract and why. This is not always an easy task and requires avoiding wanting to please everyone in favour of serving the purpose and the people. Rather, it's about creating an attractive leadership image, thereby becoming a hub within the network and attracting resources. This, in turn, requires that the leader be authentic and represent a clear purpose, guided always by the organization's values. When the official values match those that are actually lived in the organization

– great. When, as in most organizations, this match is not perfect, however, the leader should aim to be as close as possible to the values the organization actually lives without contradicting the official version.

Similarly, branding does not imply a hard-selling approach on the part of the leader. Rather, it's about creating visibility around an authentic and wholesome profile, with all the comfortable and possibly less comfortable aspects of the individual person within the specific professional context. Instead of making large efforts to sell her project to potential followers, a leader should motivate others to follow her by showing that she understands their needs: What do you need in order to perform in my team?

Leadership branding doesn't mean selling

The added layer of complexity in the network organization is that this personal brand must come across online (see online identity in chapter "Mastering technologies and creating online leadership identity", p. 122). Being present online requires that the leader show himself in a way that he becomes recognizable online. The best example for this is a person's very personal, authentic style of communicating. Through communication, a leader acknowledges and cares for the people who follow him. This includes asking how they are, showing authentic interest in their thoughts and feelings as they relate to working together, and being able to give effective feedback and motivate them.

Showing the brand online

Showing herself online also requires that the leader set boundaries and be able to say No when necessary. The goal is not to create unproductive large social networks by taking on every project and every person regardless, but to clearly target followers who are in a position to add value to the purpose. And for that, the leader must determine and communicate what the added value from her work is.

Leandro Baghdadi describes his very personal leadership brand in his interview (p. 233). He places great importance on having daily chats with all members of his team to keep the communication flowing. To accommodate his people's communication needs, Leandro finds out their individual preferences for communicating with him and tries to accommodate these. He also emphasizes reliability in doing his best to respect meeting times and agendas in an environment that is characterized by what he describes as a Latin American "sense of urgency".

Creating personal leadership branding

Personal leadership branding is a conscious and continuous process. Creating a personal style or brand of leading requires constant self-reflection on the part of the leader. In order to attract followers, he must understand the unique added value that he brings to his work and that defines his contribution. This can be, for instance, the ability to develop ideas or concepts to solve a task or problem in an innovative way. It can also be the willingness and ability to absorb risks when the team is exploring a new path where certain moves might lead to failure. The unique value a person adds often embodies the driving force behind her actions. Adding this specific value to an organization or a project motivates her. It is what she knows and enjoys doing. It is a main ingredient of her personal leadership branding.

Think of leaders you do and do not want to follow. The ones you are attracted to often have clear leadership brands. Spend some time to look at leaders around you and observe what makes you want to follow someone or not.

In the following, we offer some coaching questions to help you reflect on your personal leadership branding.

Coaching exercises

Exercise: Identify and rank your values

In this exercise, you create a set of values that are important to you.

Write each value on a card and lay them out in front of you. Then take one card after another and compare it with the following one, asking yourself: Which of the two is more important to me? Put the less important one underneath the more important one.

If you'd like to do this exercise in a more structured way, use this link: http://www.stevepavlina.com/articles/list-of-values.htm to identify your values and then rank them or directly go to http://www.value-test.com/.

Exercise: What do I stand for as a leader?

Take a moment to write down what you stand for as a leader. This could be, for example:

I very often attract global projects.

I very often attract projects where high-level customers are involved.

My way of working is very structured.

The ideas and solutions I have can be easily understood and written down on one page.

My vision is to contribute to solutions that increase the acceptance of a certain technology within society.

It might help in this exercise to reflect on your personal leadership strengths (possibly using one of the existing diagnostic tools on the market), and to identify and reflect on situations when you successfully applied these strengths in your professional career.

Exhibit 2.1: Personal branding kick-off

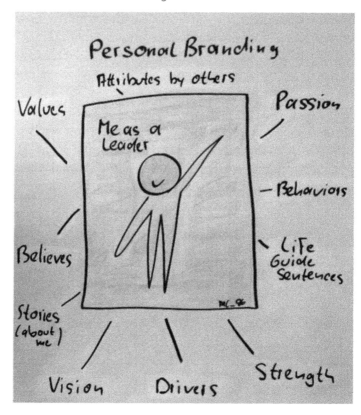

Exercise: Exploring personal qualities, challenges and resources for developing a vision*

This exercise has two parts, an individual part and a tandem work part. Before you start with the individual work make sure to find a tandem partner to do the exercise with you.

Step One: Present State

a) Individual work (invest about 15 minutes): What are my personal inner resources such as strengths, believes, etc.?

Think about your leadership initiatives in the last months and the response or feedback you have received from your peers or superiors. Then answer the following.

What are my potentials, my strengths, my (core) competences and my qualities that I can harness to achieve my vision?

Select an item that represents you as a person. Now select items that represent your potentials, (core) competences, strengths and qualities, which could be important to achieve your vision. Use the picture below as an inspiration.

---

* This exercise was developed by Bettina Schaefer, Karin Lorentz, Dorothea Schuetze and Marcus Hildebrandt. Exercise from the training "Schulen und andere Bildungseinrichtungen erfolgreich begleiten", conducted by proSchule.

Exhibit 2.2: Items to choose from

Place the item that represents you as a person in the middle and group the other symbols around it, paying attention to the meaning of distance. Closeness and distance can represent the intensity of a certain quality, personal relevance, passion, frequency of application, or something else.

Take a photo of this installation/picture (it can change at a later stage).

The images below are examples of this exercise from our workshops.

Exhibit 2.3: Personal constellation 1

Exhibit 2.4: Personal constellation 2

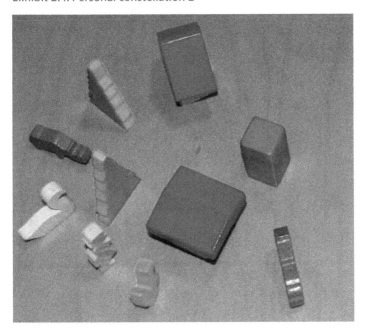

b) Tandem work (invest about 15 minutes per person): Explore and reflect the current state.

When both partners have finished creating their installations/pictures, decide whose installation to discuss first and ask the other person questions like:

What do the symbols represent?

What do you associate with them?

What meaning has...?

It is also possible to share an observation: I observe that... before asking another question.

Then switch.

Important note:

No interpretations.

Only „I"-messages.

No advices/suggestions.

Step Two: Target State (invest 15 minutes per person)

What would you like to change or develop?

Compare your present state with your future vision. Do you feel that something needs to be changed for you to be well equipped on your journey towards realizing your vision? What has to be changed or developed?

Make these changes in your installation/picture (and take a photo).

This could mean:

Move items closer or further away from the middle.

Take items away.

Introduce new items into the installation/picture.

Etc.

Your tandem partner will accompany you in this process and ask questions. They will note or sketch your answers with key words and hand you the document after the exercise.

Questions can include:

Would you like to change anything in your installation/picture? What would you like to change? Is anything missing, or would you like to move anything closer to you/to the middle?

What is different now? (Description/meaning of change.)

What conclusions do you draw from that? ("Moving closer means to me…")

What could help you to achieve this change while working towards your vision?

Exercise: Four-step model for personal branding:

In our work with global leaders, we have developed a step-by-step model for personal branding:

Ask yourself/write down/ask your team:

1. *What do I deliver?*

Please take time to reflect deeply and honestly: What do I like to do? Which added value can I bring? What are the topics that I burn for? What settings do I like to work in? Why should a company hire me? What are the outputs I create/deliver?

2. *How do I deliver this output?*

Please take time to reflect deeply and honestly: Who am I in a larger organizational/business context? What do I stand for and how can others see this in my actions? What are some characteristics that define me as a leader in the organization? What is my view of the organization? What is my view of the larger frame in which we work, including our customers, our markets, etc.? What does success mean to me? What is my perspective on teamwork? What is the best thing we can achieve together? What should definitely not happen?

You can also ask others to describe what working with you is like.

3. *What are the topics?*

Please take time to reflect deeply and honestly: Where are my areas of competence? What are the topics I like to explore deeply? What do I like in my present job? Who is my hero with regard to knowledge?

4. Synthesize 1, 2 and 3 into your personal leadership branding

Identify your personal leadership logo/tagline:

If you described your leadership style as a symbol, what would it be and why?

If you wanted to express the essence of your leadership style in a tagline, slogan or motto with no more than 12 words in no more than two sentences, what would it be? Would others understand the deeper connotation of this symbol or motto? What can you do to depict or formulate this as clearly as possible to make it catchy for others?

Remember: This exercise is not intended to help you sell yourself. Exposing yourself so consciously and openly might be a challenge depending on the national or organizational cultural background. We therefore invite you to adapt this exercise to your needs and orientations.

We have decided not to give examples for individual brands to avoid the impression there is a one-size-fits-all recipe for how to do this. Leadership brands are individual and unique. The most important thing is that your branding is visible through your actions. To illustrate this, we present you below with quotes from six CEOs or board members. They were asked to describe what leadership means to them. The quotes demonstrate that these leaders have very different brands. By reading through the quotes you may be more attracted by some of them or even repelled by others. That's exactly the point of branding.

"I lead my teams by motivation, consequence, fairness, and trustworthiness, but it is important to say, it is all nothing without passion." – Prof. Michael Bargende, Chair for Automotive Powertrains, University of Stuttgart

"I strongly believe that people make the difference. So, it's also leading by example, but also creating a good working environment for our people in terms of getting them in a position where they are challenged, make sure that they feel that they are contributing, and make sure that they feel that they have to deliver." – Jos Smetsers, Board of Management, Daf Trucks

"Successful leadership is based on professional competence, trust and empathy and the ability to adapt to different leadership situations. Expectations and goals have to be communicated mutually and clearly and they have to be reviewed constantly." – Roland Grimmelsmann, CEO Verlag Herder GmbH

"First of all, to lead people means you have to be a role model. You have to show the people what you expect from them, and you have to describe it and live it every day." – Hartmut Jenner, Kärcher Group, CEO

"For me, the core of good leadership and high performance is trust and mutual respect. Trust only works in both directions – leadership that trusts, and trust in leadership. Trust only grows where there is transparency. Trust is also the basis for good teamwork." – Klaus Rosenfeld, Schäffler Group, CEO

"Imagine a culture where employees think out of the box, where they are not afraid to speak up, and where they openly discuss and generate ideas together. First and foremost, trust in our employees, try to be a role model in living our four corporate values every day" – Elmar Degenhart, Continental, CEO

Exercise: Leaders learn from leaders

a) Think of three to five leaders in your organization who you would want to follow. What do they do that makes you want to follow them? Identify their personal leadership brand: What is unique and typical for them? How are they recognizable (both face-to-face and online)?

b) Now think of three to five leaders in your organization who you wouldn't want to follow. Why not?

c) Please think about why you would like to follow a leader. Come up with leadership characteristics that are attractive for you. For example:

He/she is very structured.
He/she knows a lot about xyz.
He/she uses their network.
He/she challenges me.

These are only examples. Remember that no two people are attracted to the same things, so your list can be completely different.

d) Please think about why you don't want to follow a leader. Now try to identify less attractive leadership characteristics. For example:

He/she comes across as impersonal.
He/she doesn't listen to me.
He/she micro-manages everything.
He/she spends too little time with the team.
Again, feel free to come up with your own characteristics.

Summary

In the network organization, followers decide what constitutes good leadership. In order to attract the right followers for her project, the leader needs to ensure her attractiveness as a leader, showing what working with her is like and investing continuously in self-reflection. In doing so, she creates her very own, unique leadership brand that shows what she stands for as a leader – a constant and continuous process. Rather than selling herself, however, the leader creates her brand by being authentic and motivating her people to follow her, ensuring they have what they need to perform well.

Contextual leadership

Interview with Arnulf Keese

VP & General Manager at PayPal (Germany, Austria and Switzerland)

Figure 2.8: Arnulf Keese's complexity image

Profile
- ❖ Vice President & General Manager at PayPal for Germany, Austria and Switzerland
- ❖ German
- ❖ 47 years old
- ❖ Married, three children
- ❖ Responsible for 200 people on site in Berlin and connected with over 2,000 worldwide

Do what you like! This is Arnulf Keese's advice to the young. "I do things that I have fun doing because I'm only good when I enjoy what I'm doing. If you don't follow your passion you lose your sleep over something you don't enjoy", is how he describes his take on work. For the past nine years, Arnulf Keese has been doing something he really likes for a living. He has helped build PayPal into a leading digital payment brand in Germany, Austria and Switzerland. This has led to great personal success. When he started nine years ago, the PayPal office counted 15 people, including more than ten temporary staff from outsourcing companies. Today, his business unit has 200 people, plus the support of 2,000 people spread across the globe!

From her work with Arnulf, Line Jehle knows that he is curious and an inspiration to other people who can easily relate to him. At the same time, he is pragmatic and skilled at simplifying problems and tasks and quick to decide according to priorities. Arnulf is goal-oriented and knows what he is talking about. Asked to describe himself, he says, "I bring it down to crisp headlines that people can relate to. I speak too much but I'm probably not too boring. I'm good at moving people and topics and teams."

Arnulf believes that, "feedback is something you need to earn". He therefore places great importance on creating continuous dialogue with his people.

The complexity wherein Arnulf operates

Arnulf is responsible for 200 people on-site in Berlin and connected to over 2,000 people worldwide.

He describes PayPal as 90% network. To underline his estimation, he explains that official reporting lines hardly have any significance in the daily operations of PayPal.

More than half of the people in his office don't report to him. If PayPal were following reporting lines, he would have to seek approval from the US head office whenever he wants them to do work for him, which is often. Clearly, this isn't practicable. Therefore, "I need to influence them to get things done. I have to influence them every single day. I convince someone else to be as convinced as I could be to want something that is in our interest. If I can prove to him, in a very genuine way, that there is a common denominator for his and my needs by doing something that serves us both."

Arnulf describes PayPal as a very agile environment that still embraces the very spirit of start-up culture. Part of this is the credo to think out of the box in a cross-functional and open way. "It's a free and innovative world characterized by playfulness. On the other hand, it is rather chaotic." Arnulf muses that he couldn't function in a traditional corporate environment, he would feel out of place in hierarchical structures. PayPal is a non-hierarchical organization that places no age limits on advancing one's career. "Our people are intrinsically driven; they appreciate the luxury to do at work what they really like doing. Performance is fuelled by this deep intrinsic motivation."

The downside of the network, Arnulf continues, is that it's like a huge party where everybody talks to everyone. "It comes at the cost of communication. My weakest point is my voice, I have a sore throat at the end of the day because I communicated all day long." In this environment, communication gets more complex as so many different layers are added. "Attractiveness is one of our biggest challenges: There are so many shiny things that it's easy to lose focus. There is a lot more inspiration around than we have means to realize. So we must prioritize."

Arnulf's strategies to reduce and navigate this complexity: What has worked and what hasn't worked so well, and why?

In order to overcome this challenge, Arnulf explains the bubble sorting method that is used in computer programming to illustrate his point. Think of ideas as bubbles in fizzy water: The bigger the bubble the faster it moves to the surface and becomes visible. In the image below, bubble/project A is given more importance and thus resources and priority than bubble/project C. While some bubbles always stay behind and never lift off of the bottom of a glass, others may need a bit longer to rise to the surface and become successful later. But rise they must.

Figure 2.9: Bubbles

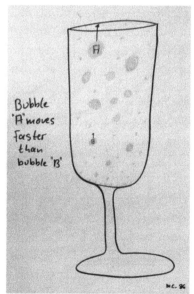

To support the rising of project bubbles, PayPal values and encourages an open communication culture highly. "I measure success by the amount of controversial comments. Controversial comments are the greatest sign of success because it signals that people haven't checked out of the process. If they no longer express their opinions, they have checked out. So I measure success by asking, are people willing to engage and voice their frustration?" Not all cultures and generations support being so outspoken, however. This can sometimes be difficult for Arnulf as he expects his people to challenge his ideas.

In order to limit objections and also get a handle on the sheer overflow of creative ideas at PayPal, they subscribe to the "Object, object, commit" rule. It expresses the "principle that a person can object twice but if his or her idea isn't picked up after the second time, he or she is expected to commit to the decision, stop resisting and go with the flow". Arnulf makes a crucial point here: "Hear everyone out! In many instances, it's not so much important that one's opinion is being followed but rather, that it's heard. Most people will support the decision made afterwards (even if it's random) even if they all have different opinions. They wouldn't if they weren't heard out. The reason is this: the expression of thought is more important than having the group follow the thought. We can live with the group not following it but we cannot live with the group not listening. So we tell our people, please share your opinion. We won't be able to turn things upside down because you disagree, but we really do care hearing your opinion. You have the privilege to be heard but you don't have the privilege to always be followed."

Arnulf describes the main task of the PayPal management team as creating, driving and maintaining a "tribal moment" for the group – a feeling of belonging and closeness. "We are all part of several groups. We are part of a tribe, such as the finance or legal team. Then there are neighbouring groups that can still be part of the same tribe. It's a bit like global circles. Everyone can be in as many circles as they want to be. You can object that it becomes arbitrary and there is no longer a binding element, but the tribe has one central binding element: culture. Shared values and rituals that describe core functions of society. Each team has its own culture. Sales people are different from marketing people. Still we invest every year in creating a tribal moment for all to foster social bonding. A mix of hard work and lots of fun."

When asked how PayPal measures the success of the tribes, Arnulf says, "I feel it." He finds attempts to measure intangible things like engagement levels in a matrix difficult. Rather, he asks, "How willing are people to go the extra mile? How much do their eyes glow when they talk about their project? It's many small things, they become much more visible when they're absent. If we had a Facebook for employees, we could measure by the density of their network connections."

Arnulf's reactions to the central parameters of leading in the face of hyper-complexity

- Shaping and influencing organizational communities – Yes. This is the biggest challenge, but also the greatest success factor.

- Creating a culture of voicing and feedback – Yes. Managers have to earn feedback.

- Dealing with complexity – Yes. I think of it more as ambiguity.

- Competence of not knowing – Yes. We need to train our instincts and learn how to deal with the unknown. I call it the "qualified gut".

- Personal branding – Yes. Define clearly what you stand for. Authenticity is the most important. You really have to believe in what you say and stand up for it.

- Contextual leadership – Yes. It's about agility and reacting to signals. Steer and adjust. When dealing with people, plan a lot of things that won't happen.

- Framework setting and mastering technology – Yes. Technology is really gadgets and we haven't really optimized them yet. They still cut out important communication and fool us by not working as we need it to and becoming outdated fast, like email.

Contextual leadership

Most of us were trained in a variety of well-established leadership models. While most of these models make a lot of sense in theory, they often fall short in the reality of global complexity. This is partly due to the fact that they usually focus on tasks and roles. A good example for this is situational leadership (see Part IV: "Some remarks about situational and contextual leadership", p. 278). While this concept works well in family-like and matrix-like organizational contexts, it regularly fails in network contexts.

In one of our leadership workshops, an experienced manager recently approached us with the following observation. "I have used situational leadership for a long time but with my new global team I have no clue how to apply it. There is not a single task that is assigned solely to one person and we don't really have a clear picture of the different roles team members hold because things change so fast. It is virtually impossible to plan a leadership intervention meticulously and then execute it. Instead, I just muddle my way through."

Situational leadership no longer suffices in hyper-complexity

Our answer: Welcome to contextual leadership!

Arnulf Keese is a good example of a contextual leader. He thinks of the people in his organizations as "tribes" – groups that find each other according to organizational contexts. He understands his task as a leader to be agile in thinking and doing, reacting to signals from his environment as they show up. He describes his take on contextual leadership as "steer and adjust". He knows that human interaction is fluid and can be unpredictable, requiring a constant probing on part of the leader.

In the preceding chapters, we have examined organizational contexts and the appropriate approaches to dealing with the corresponding levels of complexity on a more abstract level (see Part I, p. 16). We have discussed hyper-complexity and a number of methods for coping with it (see chapter "Navigating hyper-complexity", p. 39). We have shown how the principle of attractiveness guides the dynamics of networks, and how personal leadership branding attracts followers see chapter "Leadership branding", p. 65).

Aligning followers in chaotic environments

Now, we will take a look at what's necessary to align those followers to a shared purpose and motivate them to perform and stay with you. This is especially important in environments with little structure and order, where the risk of making mistakes is high. This is typical for work contexts in which business innovation and developing new business opportunities, especially in new markets, are the main objectives.

In such chaotic environments, your task is to identify from an overwhelming stream of information those weak signals that might lead to business opportunities. If you succeed in doing so, you then need to get your team on board to break new ground.

However, task management alone won't suffice to align people who are dispersed all over the world. In fact, you often won't even know what the tasks are when starting out. To have the desired impact on your people, you therefore need to attend to their local organizational environment and the dynamics – their social and cultural context – learning about their personal needs and what motivates them.

For this, in order to collect the right data and make sense of them, you need what we call contextual intelligence. Applying contextual intelligence to the realm of leading people and creating order out of chaos constitutes contextual leadership, the focus of this chapter.

The concept of contextual leadership

Contextual leadership was coined in the field of strategy development in emerging markets. Anthony Mayo and Nitin Nohria[*] characterized contextual leadership as the "ability to understand an evolving environment, and to capitalize on those evolving trends."

Defining
contextual
leadership

This definition fits perfectly our metaphor of the paramecium (p. 33) that explores its environment for new growth opportunities. Through immersion in the context, weak yet promising signals are identified in the environment. Self-organization and the flow of the environment will then enable efficient moves in the right direction.

In the following, we will apply this concept to the level of individual managers whose task is to shape and influence their networks and lead people towards creating innovation and high performance.

With this in mind, we follow the authors of http://www.business-leadership-qualitites.com who claim that "contextual leaders are those that are able to bring order out of chaos. They are able to create patterns of attention and develop networks. Contextual leaders may complement transformational leaders by

- using knowledge and information to guide actions,
- developing internal and external networks,
- fostering innovative performance."

Of course, attention to context isn't a new leadership

---

*   Mayo, Nohria (2005).

Moving away from task orientation and towards contextual intelligence

skill. However, we agree with these authors that a paradigm shift is needed. In the network, HR people and managers need to move away from the principle of task orientation, efficiency and team project management – "We have to get this done" – towards creating and using contextual intelligence to manage individuals and their environments for innovation and high performance. Contextual leadership takes on significant importance in hyper-complex network organizations. It is our aim to motivate leaders to adapt contextual leadership as their strategy and style of choice rather than a fallback option.

In the following we will take a closer look at:

- How to shift from task orientation to managing individuals in a given context;

- How to describe such context; and

- What contextual intelligence and contextual leadership mean in practical terms.

Leading in network contexts

Contextual leadership is about knowing what to do when there's no one telling you what to do

In a nutshell, contextual leadership can be summarized like this. Immerse yourself in the context. Probe and sense the context through observation and using your internal resources such as intuition, gut feeling etc. Deal professionally with the unknown. Then act. Then analyze again and adjust while you are in the situation according to what is appropriate and necessary right there and then (see Part IV: "Some remarks about situational and contextual leadership", p. 278). Contextual Leadership is about knowing what to do when there's no one telling you what to do. Makes sense, right?

As successful global managers, you are most likely already applying contextual leadership. It often happens automatically when interacting with employees. Often managers revert to contextual leadership when they feel that their tested approach to leading doesn't seem to have the desired impact. They then adapt their behaviour and try new approaches hoping that these will bring the desired responses.

In machine-like organizations, leaders are recognized for their ability to come up with a rational model to optimize the efficiency of processes and to overcome certain challenges. These challenges typically present themselves only in one geographical location of the same time zone and mostly within a singular culture.

Leaders are recognized for different abilities in the machine-like and in the network-like organization

In the network organization, on the other hand, challenges are of international or global dimensions. People work together across borders, time zones, organizational structures and cultures. Roles and tasks can be very fuzzy or even substituted by person-specific identities and the purpose of one's contribution to the organization. Roles and tasks may be understood differently due to different cultural and local perspectives and agendas. Moreover, power in the network works differently. Control and coercion as leadership instruments based on physical co-location lose importance because of the absence of daily face-to-face interaction. Power must be exercised through an active effort on part of the leader to create work environments that attract people.

In the introductory example at the beginning of this chapter, situational leadership is failing chiefly because the leader isn't able to assign single tasks to individuals. Instead, the tasks are of a complexity that demands the attention of several people. Very often these people are not even members of the same global team. Task assignment may therefore have a limited impact at best.

In networks and communities, the purpose of collaboration is spread across dispersed groups

In such an environment, the leader often neither has the power nor sufficient knowledge to assign clear tasks or give clear orders. And so the basic assumptions of situational leadership – that the tasks are known and that they can be clearly assigned to one person – no longer hold in communities and networks. Here, the purpose of collaboration is spread across dispersed groups. The delivery of work packages usually depends on employees or small sub networks whose links to other group members are weak.

Against this background, ask yourself: Why would you work for someone you don't know and for a purpose that's not obviously yours when you don't even know whether this collaboration will help your local career?

It is because of this that a shift in thinking becomes increasingly important, away from the task and towards the people that are needed to get things moving.

In consequence, contextual leadership enables impacting and influencing people by taking into account the whole context of a situation and/or a person by asking:

- How are they embedded within the team and the network? and

- How could they and their interactions with others be influenced?

The two skills dimensions of the contextual leader

It follows that the contextual leader is skilled in reading and responding in two contextual dimensions:

- The people with whom she interacts; and

- The environment in which she acts and its dynamics.

A leader may realize, for example, that the local environment of one team member is so demanding that this person has to prioritize local demands and won't be able to fully serve the global purpose. In this case local power is so strong that the leader has to think about alternative strategies or solutions to get things done. One option could be to influence the superiors of the local team member. Another option is for the leader to convince the person that he will carry the full risk of the initiative and make sure that team members' good performance will be recognized by the organization.

The challenge in the network is that due to hyper-complexity, situations differ too much to be solved by the same approach implemented in a local machine or family organization. Contextual leadership calls for great flexibility and a distinctly tailored approach to solve it.

In order to cope with the challenges of the network organization, the leader has to execute her interventions in two organizational dimensions: globally and locally. Often, conflicts in global projects arise from a lack of alignment of local and global purposes and priorities. It is therefore important that the leader includes local decision-makers in his global network, enters into an ongoing dialogue with them, ensures that the global project is included in local objectives, and creates an attractive framework in which people want to work.

The following (fictitious) job description mirrors all this.

WANTED

A Network Leader with situational, transformational, and team leader qualities. He or she will have the following profile.

WANTED: A job description for the network leader

- You are a servant–leader, facilitator and advisor who works collaboratively with team members and knows how to delegate. You have integrity and strong ethical values. You are able to "check your ego at the door". If you are driven by the need for power and control, this will not be the right environment for you. If you want to take responsibility and contribute to your team and the organization's success, you have come to the right place.

- You have exceptional conceptual and emotional intelligence which you use to manage a hyper-complex network in an organization characterized by geographical distance, organizational and cultural boundaries and communication technology unknown to 20th-century leaders.

- You are committed to life-long learning and able to learn as well as teach in a virtual learning environment.

- You are an excellent communicator who is able to build and maintain rapport and create a positive working and learning environment.

- You are able to share your and the organization's collective vision, motivate, communicate, appraise and encourage people – all remotely.

- You have well-developed global business skills and sound experience in managing multicultural groups that consist of individuals both within and outside of your core team. Team members and groups will be overlapping and changing constantly to meet the needs of a dynamic customer base dispersed throughout the world.

- You are technically capable and able to measure not only the "hard" facts of business performance but also the "soft" facts that indicate qualitative improvements of services and people.

If you meet these criteria, please apply at your nearest global organization. They may not know it yet, but they need you badly.

This ad is fictitious. For a real-life competency description advertised by a large global company, please see the next page.

Implementing contextual leadership: The "Contextual Intelligence Framework"

As mentioned above, implementing contextual leadership requires a shift in perspective away from the task and toward the person and their context while using one's instruments without thinking about it.

Our findings match those of Tammy Erickson[*] of the London Business School who has found that, "Today, leadership is less about being the best than about creating a context in which others can succeed".

Contextual leadership is about:

- Creating a purpose-oriented and shared space for global cooperation which fosters innovation (see chapter "Mastering technologies and creating online leadership identity", p. 122).

- Appreciating and exploiting diversity rather than levelling it out[†].

- Being immersed in the context when solving problems and making decisions.

- Probing the environment for responses to challenging leadership initiatives that strive for innovation and new business opportunities (see chapter "Navigating hyper-complexity", p. 39).

- Creating a sense of belonging through personal branding, sense-making and framework setting (see chapters "Leadership branding", p. 65, and "Mastering technologies and creating online leadership identity", p. 122).

---

[*] http://www.forbes.com/sites/lbsbusinessstrategyreview/ 2014/02/07/developing-contextual-leaders/.

[†] Hildebrandt et al. (2013), chapter 1.

How does one develop the skills needed for contextual leadership? Through acquiring or improving network and community competences. Creating networks and supporting the corresponding connections across the organization* is key to honing one's contextual leadership skills. Network and community management is no longer something that can be relegated to managers' spare time outside of their core work programme.†

Here is an internal competence profile from a large global company for Social Business Community Managers.

Competence profile: Social Business Community Manager (internal CM)

Basic abilities and characteristics:
Flexible
Stress resistant
Empathic
Team player
Passionate, motivated, involved
Diplomatic
Knows company workflow and processes
E2.0/social media evangelist
Web aficionado (has an online life and uses web functions and mechanisms actively)
Networker
Extroverted, open
Assertive
Loves to learn

---

*   See Part IV: "The concepts of groups, networks and communities", p. 269, for further information on the role of hubs and weak links in networks and communities.

†   To better reflect reality, BOSCH has been working with their managers to shift their focus from teams to communities as the basic organizational unit. See for example https://www.youtube.com/watch?v=M5KKmzH7INg, available only in German.

Skills:

Table 2.2: Skills

Technical and functional skills	• Tool knowledge (Connect, Portal, Web) • Thematic knowledge (functional area) • Legal knowledge (Web) • Generates and edits content • (agile) Project management • Change Management
Methodological skills	• Organizing (including events on-/offline) (2) • Web analyst (reporting, monitoring, KPI) (2) • Creativity / innovation / presentation (2) • Crisis communication / mediation (3) • Moderation (virtual) (3) • Training others (3) • Knowledge management (2) • Thinks conceptually (2)
Social skills	• Team player (3) • Empathic (3) • Loves to learn (3) • Extroverted (3) • Stress resistant (3) • Self management (3) • Interculturally sensitive (3)
Leadership skills	• Develops people and supports them in gaining targets (2) • Transformational leader (2) • Applies Social Business Principles (2)
Entrepreneurial skills	• Detects trends (2) • Analyzes, identifies, engages target audiences (2) • Entrepreneurship (1) • Explorative approach to business

Moreover, contextual leadership requires a high level of contextual intelligence that takes human behaviours and systems dynamics into account.

Matthew Kutz defines contextual intelligence as follows: *"Contextual intelligence is the ability to quickly and intuitively recognize and diagnose the dynamic contextual*

Contextual intelligence defined

variables inherent in an event or circumstance and results in intentional adjustment of behaviour in order to exert appropriate influence in that context. * "

Let's have a closer look at the two words **context** and **intelligence**.

Intelligence

Intelligence is a word that has very different connotations and meanings in different cultures. The ontological and epistemological origins of intelligence are highly debated. For our purpose, suffice it to consider a definition on WordNet®: "Intelligence is the ability to comprehend; to understand and profit from experience." † According to this, intelligence denotes the ability to transform data into useful information through interpretation, information into knowledge by taking the context into account, and knowledge into practice by applying the knowledge to our actions.

Intercultural intelligence

Applied to "intercultural intelligence" this definition denotes the competence to adapt processes and communication to different international interfaces and make these competences an active part of one's leadership portfolio. Taking this one step further, we believe that in the face of hyper-complexity transcultural intelligence is needed, meaning the ability to co-create attractive, often virtual (work-)spaces that openly employ diversity and transcend it.

Context

Context consists of all the external, internal, interpersonal and intrapersonal factors that contribute to the uniqueness of each situation and circumstance.

Contextual intelligence

With these definitions in place, let's now approach the concept of contextual intelligence.

---

*   Kutz (2008).

†   http://wordnetweb.princeton.edu/perl/webwn?s=intelligence&sub=Search+WordNet&o2=&o0=1&o8=1&o1=1&o7=&o5=&o9=&o6=&o3=&o4=&h=.

Developing your contextual intelligence means translating data into useful knowledge by using the context as the frame for making sense of the information. This requires that you be constantly embedded in what is going on, immersed in all information and communication streams. In order to achieve that you have to interact, interact and interact with all relevant network members and use the interactions to read and understand the unique context wherein each of them is embedded.

Immersion in the context: interact, interact, interact

Here is what you do:

- Enter the situation.

- Collect context data.

- Try out an action.

- Assess the reaction.

- Collect new context data.

- Adjust.

- Try again.

- Assess the reaction.

- Collect new context data.

- Adjust.

- Try again.

- And so on and so on.........it never stops!

We believe that new leadership approaches should go hand in hand with new ways of leadership development and tailor-made solutions in supporting. Thus we are in the process of transferring the concept of "being immersed", contextual intelligence and creating closeness at a distance also to the fields of e-learning and especially to e-coaching. We have included in the last part of the

'Away' and 'toward' reactions

book some ideas around these topics (see Part IV: "New approaches to coaching: Immersive Coaching", p. 306).

To evaluate the reaction of your environment to your leadership initiative we suggest a simple concept. Look for the 'away' or 'toward' reactions. In other words, do your actions create a 'toward' or an 'away' behaviour on part of the people around you?

However, 'toward' doesn't necessarily mean that you get positive responses or even elaborate feedback on your initiatives. Rather, recognize it by observing whether there is intense discussion of your ideas, with positive and negative reactions signalling that you made an impact; or whether your initiative is ignored and the environment remains silent.

Unlocking the context

Let's now take a closer look at the context itself. How can it be described? What constitutes context? Due to its very nature, hyper-complexity doesn't lend itself to a generic definition of context relevant for leadership initiatives. Instead, it's useful to share different areas of context that may influence situations. In the following, we suggest some questions you can ask yourself and the people around you when you are in a situation that shows all facets of your context.

The context can require leadership attention in two dimensions:

- The **person** you interact with; and
- The **environment** and its **dynamics** in which the person is **embedded**.

The person

1. <u>The person</u>

- What is their personality?
- What might guide their actions? What is their cultural context?

- To which generation do they belong? Baby boomers, X, Y or Z (see Part IV: "Some remarks about Generation Y", p. 277)?

- What motivates them?

- What is their understanding of success and career?

- What are their personal long-term goals?

- Do personal, intimate beliefs such as religion play a role?

- Which competences do they have?

- What is their private situation like?

- To which networks do they belong? By which networks are they influenced?

- What are their problem-solving competences and self-organization skills?

2. <u>Environment and dynamics</u>

- In which context (function, role, etc.) does the person operate?

The environment and its dynamics

- How can the complexity mix be described (percentages on family, machine and network; see Part I, p. 16, 24)? What percentage of their total work time does the person spend in the network?

- What is the organizational structure relevant to the context?

- Does the local structure support the network project?

- How clearly is the purpose of the cooperation defined?

- In which organizational and cultural language is the purpose defined?

- Is the purpose in conflict with local organizational requirements?

- Does the local environment have a long tradition of working globally or is this relatively new?

- What happens in the external environment and how does this influence the person's context (fluctuation of staff, job market, recession, etc.)?

- How can the dynamics impacting the person and the local context be described? What are possible attractors (people, initiatives etc.) that influence the dynamics? Are there possible trends, projects or initiatives that show weak but promising signs for future success?

- What are the hubs and weak links connected to the local environment?

Of course reality is not an objective and absolute concept but subject to individual perception. So is context. We process context and try to learn from it, establishing contextual intelligence by identifying patterns or dynamic levers that can be used to influence the environment or the person. In doing so we need to be aware of our own cognitive biases and encourage this same awareness with our co-workers to remain open to differing perceptions of the context. Hence describing a context to another person means giving them clues about how your perception of the world is influenced by your own biography and cultural embedding. This can only be achieved through self-reflection and sharing the resulting insights with others.

Cultural filters

All description of context and personality is directly and indirectly influenced by cultural filters, amongst other factors. If I come from a traditional Japanese office worker background I may perceive the constant subtle joking of my British superior inappropriate in the context, while the British superior might perceive the Japanese team member as lacking humour. However, neither assumption implies either person does or does not have humour.

A first step toward becoming more aware of one's cultural filters is asking others how they perceive the individual and others in the group. This should always be done carefully and in a one-on-one setting (see chapter "Shaping global dialogue", p. 159). Second, a vast bulk of research and literature exists in the intercultural field, which helps us reflect on our own cultural imprints. [*]

The absence of pre-defined, generic solutions makes contextual leadership particularly appropriate and successful in culturally complex work environments. Rather than responding to "the Americans" or "the Chinese" on the basis of mere generalized assumptions about these cultures, the leader has the duty and the luxury to respond to the individual persons and impulses. His response will be based on his relevant knowledge and experience acquired over years of practice and self-reflection but will not seek to replicate or transplant solutions out of context. Remember the improvising jazz musician.

Here are some tips for training and improving your and your co-workers' contextual intelligence.

Training your contextual intelligence

- Keep adding to your toolbox for complex problem-solving:
  - Provide sufficient opportunities to jointly try to make sense of the usual data overload by creating new and creative questions around the data.
  - Use computer simulation of complex systems (best suited are simulations of organizations in fast-evolving markets) in order to learn how to identify weak signals, attractors and dynamic levers that can be used to influence the system.
  - Share with your colleagues your perceptions of how decisions and leadership initiatives made

---

[*] House et al. (2004); Trompenaars, Hampden-Turner (2004); Meyer (2014).

an impact on people and whole organizations.
- Create a continuous flow of discussion around personal values (see also chapter "Leadership branding", p. 65):

• Get to know others' values to connect with their authentic self.

• In order for others to be and show their true self, give them time and structured support (e.g. facilitation) as appropriate. Motivate your team to leave their comfort zone together with you to discover everyone's values.

Leading with dotted lines

Leading with dotted lines

Let's look at leading with dotted lines – a context with which you may be familiar. The main challenges when leading a person with dotted lines include the following.

• It is usually not possible to apply a directive leadership style and make the person do something as the person is reporting to another, usually local, manager.

• Face-to-face contact with the person is rare.

• The person tends to be more loyal to their local context.

• The business context in which the person is embedded and relates to their manager and colleagues is often quite complex. This can either lead to unclear roles and responsibilities (in matrix contexts) or even to a complete breakdown of the concept of roles and responsibilities (for example in business networks or communities). In network contexts the notions of personal identity, purpose and attractiveness are more meaningful than roles and responsibilities.

Here are some ideas for dealing with these challenges.

Reverse management approaches, where the focus is on the person and the leader's role is that of enabler, are well suited for this kind of context. This is in direct contrast to traditional approaches where the manager is the centre of the work universe and the co-workers' role is to enable the manager to achieve his or her leadership goals. If this is done successfully, the co-workers will receive their full salary in return (transactional leadership).

A first step toward reverse management is applying transformational leadership, customized to the needs of the individual co-worker. Coaching and mentoring are great tools to achieve this. In this realm, leadership initiatives should create a force field of attractiveness that pulls the co-worker toward collaborating with the manager and the other group members.

Ask yourself: Is my leadership branding (my value propositions and the benefits of working for me, etc.; see chapter "Leadership branding", p. 65) attractive and meaningful enough to motivate co-workers to follow me? Do they feel that who they are and what they need is seen?

This is the individual side of creating a pull away from the local context towards the global context.

The other side is framework setting. Here the main challenge is creating or improving a purple space* that makes it attractive for the co-worker to collaborate with all group members in their business context.[†]

Finally, here are some ideas for dealing with complex

Reverse Management

Agile Project Management

---

*   Hildebrandt et al. (2013), chapter 1.

†   For further details on this concept see chapter "Mastering technologies and creating online leadership identity", p. 122.

collaboration environments. One way is applying agile project management to cope with the speed of changes in the environment and with unclear directions.

If you are embedded in a matrix environment you will need to enable the success factors of the organizational form.

- Together with all group members, create a chart showing: Which are the main/critical work packages/processes? Who is accountable? Who is responsible? Who is involved in decision-making? Who has a veto right? Who should be informed? etc.

- Develop clear guidelines (Governance Principles) for solving conflicts that occur naturally in matrix organizations (e.g. Flexibility versus Standardization, Quality versus Time to Market, etc.).

- Establish shared leadership and promote self-organization to help people take the whole picture into account and take more responsibility.

- Define clear escalation lines and principles and delegate to the right level of responsibility.

Letting go of steering and controlling is key

In the case of a complex network, letting go of steering and controlling through roles and responsibilities is key. Rather, leaders manage hubs – the central knots in the system – and identify and promote the emerging attractors by providing a framework for self-organization. This includes a shared purpose of collaborating as well as a shared identity for the network or community (see Part IV: "The concepts of groups, networks and communities, p. 269, for further information on this).

Exercises

The following exercise is meant to simulate context and stimulate your senses. Do apply the "probe, observe and adjust" technique.

The Probe-Observe-Adjust technique

Think about your own group, team or network and try to describe the different individuals in their context. Here are some examples.

Paul has been with the company for eight years, mostly working in analytical and data-based roles. He likes to analyze things and enjoys exploring information for new insights. He has been spending his entire life in Detroit and operates from the Detroit office. His core strength lies in transforming everything into numbers. He loves details and is the first to spot errors and inaccuracies. He likes to work in a structured way and resists change unless it is absolutely necessary. You have noticed that he responds well when things are well prepared. He likes it when people are precise. He doesn't like people who are overly emotional or casual with important issues. He really likes stability in his relationships, which are mostly built on face-to-face interaction. He seems quite formal and reserved to you. He comes across as very thoughtful. You trust him because he is consistent and reliable. He has two children.

Faye is a very experienced worker based in Singapore. She was born in China to a Chinese mother and an Indian father. She has a very international background. Before she joined the company 12 years ago, she spent time in other Asian countries. She has worked in multiple locations and has a huge international network. She is passionate about the business and the emerging ideas. She likes to nurture others and enjoys serving the team, often guiding and supporting other team members. She is a good listener. Sometimes she focuses too much on pleasing others and maintaining harmony in the team. She is very loyal and committed but works at a more relaxed pace than others in your team, needing more time to reflect on issues and contemplate options. She is a peacemaker and enjoys consensus. She will always prioritize a human issue over getting a task done. Her relaxed nature means that she is quite patient but some see this as a lack of enthusiasm. She is not that fond of virtual collaboration and her technical skills are limited. At the moment, the Singapore office is going through a major reorganization and Faye is asked to support this project in addition to her regular workload.

Jon joined the company two years ago. He is based in your office. He is very focused on his career and has just finished an MBA in international project management. Before he joined the company he was working for one of the top ten international consultancies. He was born and raised in the Netherlands. He is decisive and focused. When seeking solutions to problems, he tends to work logically and quickly. He is action-oriented and thrives on competition. He gets things done and dislikes spending time on small talk, details or feelings. He likes people who are confident and assertive and responds best when people are direct and to the point.

How would you handle the following situations with each of these members? Would you apply the same or a different approach to each of them?

Scenarios

1. One of your project partners has approached you with the following feedback. "We are not satisfied with your response time and are finding the communication with your team member difficult."
   a. How would you approach this with Jon?
   b. How would you approach this with Paul?
   c. How would you approach this with Faye?

2. You have the feeling that you are not sufficiently informed about what is happening in the project. It may be that your team isn't spending the necessary time and energy required to perform well.
   a. How would you approach this with Faye?
   b. How would you approach this with Paul?
   c. How would you approach this with Jon?

Summary

In summary, contextual leadership calls for the ability of the leader to meet any context and work with it without applying pre-defined solutions. It means being able to react and respond to a challenge in flexible, innovative and very context-specific ways. Just like our friend, the paramecium, who defines the direction it moves into as it is moving by reacting to whatever comes up in its environment, the contextual leader acts, "feels" the context and goes along with it. This requires leaders who are able to self-reflect deeply and continuously, to self-lead efficiently and to cope with uncertainty and the unknown.

Mastering technologies and creating online leadership identity

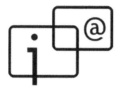

Interview with Luis Pedro Ferreira

Corporate Affairs Senior Manager at Dana

Figure 2.10: Luis Pedro Ferreira's complexity image

Profile
- ❖ Senior Manager of Corporate Affairs, South America, Dana
- ❖ Brazilian
- ❖ 48 years old
- ❖ Married, one daughter

Luis Pedro Ferreira holds a degree in Graphic Design and an MBA. He has been with Dana for 17 years with their communications department. As Corporate Affairs Senior Manager Luis is responsible for corporate communications, PR, marketing communications and government and customer relations and, whenever the company needs representation. "I represent the company in councils and trade institutions. My role is keeper of the company's image, attend trade meetings, listen, bring the business agenda in and also bring the trade agenda backwards to the company. It's a very broad activity."

The complexity wherein Luis operates

"There are two ways of describing this complexity. One is a tangle of wires. I do not really have a problem with any tangle, I know it is there and can start untangling it. However, the problem is that we do not really see or even recognise the tangle. We only see all these wires, seemingly lying just there and flat, but they are not. It is a very complex, non-confrontational environment, where people actually do not really tell what they feel. They are not really open to realizing that they do have a problem. They will tell you they are glad that you are there to help, but they are actually not, so you have to go beyond that. It is not a matter restricted to the company, it's a cultural issue. I perceive the same lack of sensibility from peers and from people in leadership positions in all countries in the region. They will tell you that there is no problem, however there is one, yet they may not see it. This not only happens in the business world, but also in politics, between governments. I guess this is part of human nature that some cultures are more open than others. However they won't slap you in the face, but try to make your life harder. As they do, they are making their own lives harder. The description of this environment is not that clear. When you look at organisations, they are trying to move in a very old-fashioned way, reluctant or failing as they publish an organisational chart with all those little boxes and those lines and dotted lines. They 'tell', 'Well, this is you and these are the guys that actually don't really report to you, but you have to work with them and they have to "report" to you.' It is very complex, not an open or clear environment, it is rather shadowy.

There is a lot of blurriness around organizations (companies, governments) and this is why I just love it. I love having to dig in and try to figure out what is really going on behind these things. I am not that keen to try to set up a plan to fool the other side. I do believe that in order to move forward with negotiation, if it's not good for both parties, or the three parties, or whatever, it's not going to happen. When I say, 'Well you have to do it, because I am telling you to', we won't progress much. I have attended a meeting that when I stepped out, I was absolutely drained. The other party was not ready to deal in a partnership mode, facing us as an opponent or as an enemy. As if we were trying to steal something from them and they needed to protect their selves. I do not only witness this in the business world, but also in our own society. People sometimes fail to realise that things should be good for all parties. Going back to how we started this bit of the conversation: A lack of proper recognition or awareness of the problems makes things harder. If you do not recognise that there is a problem, then you have two problems. That is pretty much the environment that we live in.

When I joined the company, the area that I was in had 15 people, nowadays it is just me. That means I work with agencies a lot and with different areas of the company. It is really unique to lead without having the hierarchy present. And that happens a lot when I engage with the outside world. It is very challenging to actually get people engaged and do something with you, when you are not their boss. The period of my life where I learned the most about my role, its tasks and the challenges, was when I lived in Argentina. When societies are pretty much in survival mode, people need to perceive what it is in it for them. The benefit of the whole does not really play into account."

To the question about the distribution of family, matrix and network elements at Dana, Luis responds, "I would say it is 70% machine and family and the last 30 would be network. It is evolving to something else, but it may not get down to the plant level ever. The plants are doing what they have to do and the corporate section is dealing with the network, it is another dynamic.

But I do feel that we coexist nicely with the three environments. If I am in a plant, it is pretty much family-oriented. When I go to our corporate environment, we are moving away from family, but we are still family. Sometimes we have to let colleagues go due to cost reduction activities. We grieve, because it is painful to send a friend away. We may say it is all about processes and results but we fail to realise that we do not really have a process, we have people to execute tasks that become the process. We may have to avoid dependence on people from a liability perspective.

When we move upward in organizations, they are very much network-oriented. Still there is this fixed structure with the organisational chart. So we coexist with both: the foundation is the family, the structure is moving toward the network, and there is also the matrix in the middle. Depending on how you analyse the environment, you are going to see these three environments going on. When you go to plants, you can see there is a lot of 'family'. Manufacturing companies recognize plants as the core of the whole business, it is where they make the parts that go to the customers. You have to be efficient and operationally sound. Plants shall operate under the same environment, with common KPIs to measure everything and make sense of it."

For Luis, one of the central questions resulting from this complex, global environment is how one can build trust in each other if one isn't there in person.

Luis' strategies to reduce and navigate this complexity: What has worked and what hasn't worked so well, and why?

"I am struggling with facing the fact that old practices are not working. Until recently I was able to get together with people in person, build mutual trust. This would help me to realise their needs and to do something together. Some years ago I was in a global role and it was a big failure for me. I was not able to cope with the expectations of my role, because I was not able to meet my peers and be together long enough to build a relationship. There was a reporting dotted line to me, but the responsibility was mine if things went sour. I am experiencing something similar with the team from another country right now. I have been trying to help them for about three years. This tells you all – if you try to help for three years, you are simply not helping. Phone or video are not working, much is lost in translation. There may be a hidden agenda. This has been going on and on, but it does not happen. Maybe there are a lot of cultural things in place as well, which also plays a strange ingredient with this recipe of collaboration. I think it is simultaneously exciting, frustrating and quite stressful to try to progress.

The starting point is realising that there are differences. The cultural differences are key to the success of whatever you are going to do. If you do not take this into consideration you are not going to be able to go on, unless you are working in a militaristic culture, where you are up in the hierarchy and people have to do what you say. It is about managing internal and external conflicts – this is something I do all the time. I think that the successes we were able to achieve were mostly due to fact that I realised there was something bigger beyond and invested a lot of time trying to understand it. You have to understand the environment and what is in it for all sides. It is your role to bring them together and to take away the conflict. Even if it means moving away from the family-type environment."

Luis' reactions to the central parameters of leading in the face of hyper-complexity

- <u>Shaping and influencing organizational communities</u> – Yes. It is vital that we realise that these old approaches of getting together – that good teams will actually only exist if we first know each other in person – are not valid any more. Old global organizations are facing a really hard time to realise that these communities can exist without this former approach. However we still rely on these manifestations when deploying and embracing technologies. We do have several examples where some features were based on premises that actually do not exist from personal contact. But we are still stuck in the concepts.

- <u>Creating virtual closeness and global collaboration spaces</u> – Yes. These are growing pains, not only influencing, but also being able to establish the environment to actually foster the creation of community. Organisations have a leading role and have to assume this role, but there is a conflict of interest in it. They want to benefit, but they do not really possess the knowledge, or even the DNA to actually embrace and promote this environment. This is probably the biggest problem.

- <u>Framework setting and mastering technology</u> – Yes

- <u>Dealing with complexity</u> – Yes. We need to acknowledge the complexity first in order to be able to deal with it. If you do not realise you have a problem

you have to browse. I have read a very interesting article, in the foreign issue of the Economist. They were quoting Jeffrey Immelt, the CEO for GE and successor of Jack Welch. He was saying they are trying to make matters simpler; to realise that the complex environment that companies operate in has created extra complexity. Companies have created solutions, systems and rules which are complex in themselves. They dealt with complexity by adding complexity to it, and this makes matters worse. Let's look at a the dilemma of corporate internal communication: We have 2,000 people working in a company and each one of them have their own expectations about how they want to be communicated with, how they want to be addressed, and that can change from subject to subject. For example: 1. Some may want to receive a message on their mobile about this matter; 2. About other subjects, they prefer to learn directly from their leaders; 3. Or they may prefer to read about it – if they have time. When we are considering this, we do not really know how to address this and we are stuck, we may opt for one simple solution, and fail to meet the expectations. If you communicate with them via WhatsApp, some people may feel bothered and then not be willing to be a part of it. Then they may complain about not knowing something. It is very demanding and it is yet to be seen how we are going to deal with it. It is very complex and this is why companies are going back to what Jeffrey Immelt said. He was saying there was a big gap for GE to try to make things easier and not that complex. Eventually people will – going back to the main things we have said during this conversation – have to accept that things are not working the way they are. The available options are hard for us to adopt or to embrace and I do not think it is a matter of gender or age. I think technology can connect people in a way that we have never imagined. It is all about keeping our minds open to it.

- Personal branding – Yes. We learn from experience: others assign you to a brand. This brand is built based on several manifestations that can exist in this virtual environment. This may not be true to what you perceive as yourself, but it exists, nevertheless. We have not been successful with accepting the first three items that you mentioned, let alone personal branding.

- Contextual leadership – Yes. Everyone wants to be able to customise their needs, their settings, how people react. We live in the age of "myself", where "I" matter the most. Some people get upset with their leaders, because they do not really recognise them or understand the way they should be communicated with. It is pretty much unfair and I do pity leaders, because they are facing a more and more complex environment. The environment is not that friendly, people are more demanding, there is a lot of criticism.

- Creating a culture of voicing – Yes. Here you enter a challenging environment for Latin Americans. It is very hard for people first to detach themselves from the product of their work. Feedback is very hard for us in Latin America. There is a lot of back-tapping. We all know examples of people who had problems – which makes me wonder what my problems are... Of course I have asked others about it, not only one but several, but no one is going to tell me really what my problems are – because it is hard to tell and not get personal. Voicing is being able to speak about things that upset us, or general problems. If you do not really solve these matters, eventually the bill will come in. And when it does, there is nothing you can do to learn from it. It is just gone. This could exist in any environment. I do remember one thing that a great leader that I have worked with had said. He was telling me how amazed he was with feedback sessions that he had witnessed in Germany, where they spoke openly about the problems and afterwards they went for a beer. If we said something similar to each other in South America, we would go for a fight and we would not speak to each other for years! And it is even more dramatic of a challenge when you are trying to establish this environment of openness where you do not actually see each other. Maybe if you could see each other, it would make things easier. Probably just the big outcome is: Try to embrace culture and technology in their fullness, so that we can actually take advantage.

- <u>Measuring success</u> – Yes. Let me go back to the actual definition of the word success. This requires a broader perspective. Probably if you can go beyond the short-term objectives and actually realise that you are building up something that is going to last, that it provides space for fulfilment from all parties involved, it is a good direction – but how do we measure that? The intangible is always challenging to be measured, especially when we live in this world of numbers, of CFOs and finance ruling the game. This is where I stand less hopeful, in terms of being able to measure the success. I think we have been failing to look at things in a broader way than just achieving EBITDA.

Mastering technologies and creating online leadership identity

Imagine an office where you can't small talk with your colleagues. An office where saying Good Morning to each other is not possible. Where you can't have a cup of coffee. Where you can't ask a co-worker a quick question.

Where you can't see the faces of your co-workers. Does this sound like a place where you would like to be? Probably not. But in fact, this is often the case for people who work in networks. Managers often fail to display online leadership presence and define the frame for collaboration. Equally, ensuring the technical framework is set to enable the necessary interactions is often amiss. Often, interactions are reduced to, "I want something from you".

If you as a network leader desire for your co-workers and network members to feel as close to each other as they could in co-location and interact accordingly, it is your job to role model the relevant competencies and provide the enabling online environment for such interaction.

Luis Pedro Ferreira's experience shows how much targeted and dedicated work leadership needs to invest in communicating with their people at a distance. Often, the initial barriers of technology and absence seem to be the deal breaker to nurturing global high performance. When technologies aren't optimized and their use isn't trained and customized properly, difficulties crop up quickly. The leader needs to lead by good example in showing continued online presence and motivating their groups and networks to simulate the reality of co-location online.

Why leaders are responsible for collaboration technologies

Many managers experience the task of providing the necessary technical framework and showing leadership presence online as unfamiliar and particularly challenging. Usually, digital leadership wasn't included in their education. Moreover, technology is often regarded as something we use on a basic level, in most cases without training. To most of us, our leadership responsibility to steer, set and control the available technologies or to develop and implement the desired behaviour when collaborating through media isn't obvious.

People in leadership positions tend to think of technology as something that they just use and that just has to work. We often hear from those people that they don't have the necessary technological setup to collaborate across space and time. They tend to believe that if they had a better system everything would work automatically. But this is often a big misunderstanding. Because technology by itself does not change anything at all!

Three central leadership tasks to steer, set and control technology

Against this background, we have identified three central leadership tasks in relation to technology:

1. Managing the technological framework of the network;

2. Ensuring that all network members acquire the competences required to perform within this technological framework; and

3. Role modelling efficient virtual interaction.

It's how we use and master our media that makes all the difference. And this is a leadership task. In fact, we suggest that managing and living technology makes for about 25% of the job of managing virtual, hyper-complex environments.

The concept of mastering technologies and creating online leadership presence

Furnishing and populating the virtual office

Imagine that a virtual collaboration space and the corresponding collaboration technology (e.g. a web-based conferencing tool, a shared data space and an email and calendar system) are the same as a regular office building. The mere act of buying a building doesn't guarantee that anyone will use this place for the intended purpose and that successful interactions will take place. The building itself has strengths and weaknesses and provides options but it has to be filled with real-life interactions and work processes. The Why and the What provide the shift from mere architecture to an office space: Why people want to work there and What they do there.

Hence one element of successful online collaboration is providing and framing the purpose of the virtual office where a group can interact. Developing the competences to live out the group's purpose and work inside the building is the other success factor.

In our book "Closeness at a Distance: Leading Virtual Groups to High Performance"[*], we introduced the concept of the "purple space", a transcultural, virtual space for global collaboration, where the complexity of such collaboration is reduced, which, in turn, makes it attractive for its users. Now, we would like to further refine this concept by introducing a new factor that has to be taken into account when designing such a collaboration space: What is the actual purpose of the purple space.

The purpose of the virtual office

Let's use the metaphor of the office building to illustrate what we mean. The term "office building" already implies the architectural purpose of its usage. People go there because it enables them to fulfil a work-related purpose. Applied to virtual group/network collaboration, the same is true for the virtual office building. Ask: Why are we here? And: What is the purpose for our being here and interacting inside this "building" with our network? And, finally: Is it appealing to us? The last point goes back to building attractive work environments (see chapter "Leadership branding", p. 65), where the members of the virtual group can develop a sense of belonging.

---

* Hildebrandt et al. (2013), chapters 1 and 8.

Making your virtual office an attractive place where your people enjoy being and performing has a lot to do with the choice of technologies used for interaction. Companies often have a number of software tools available that enable virtual interaction, but people are often not aware of their existence or don't feel comfortable using them. Here, our main message is this:

Think in terms of interactions and not in terms of technology.

Think in terms of interactions!

For example, ask yourself, which interactions happen automatically in a well-functioning team that works together physically in an office building but whose members occupy separate rooms? What do people do in a physical office building? Look around and observe. You may come up with the following list of possible (purpose driven!) interactions:

• Asking quick questions

• Keeping social contact

• Informing each other

• Taking decisions jointly

• Etc.

As stipulated earlier, it's the manager's job to make those interactions technologically possible and to ensure that people train and develop the necessary competences to use the technologies vividly. When a group succeeds in this, they use technology to simulate reality[*] or even "extend reality".

Patricia Anthony (see her interview on p. 245) stresses the importance of media and constant communication but she also cautions against sending too many emails and

---

[*]   Majchrzak et al. (2004).

strongly advocates to pick up the phone before over-using or relying solely on media. In order to develop relationships with people, some personal voice or face-to-face interaction is crucial in her experience.

Remember that the label or the brand of the technological system doesn't matter in the end. You don't always need high-end systems. Instead, remember the three main leadership tasks when it comes to technology:

1. Managing the technological framework of the network;

2. Ensuring that all network members acquire the competences required to perform within this technological framework; and

3. Role modelling efficient virtual interaction.

In the following section, we will look at what these tasks encompass.

How to master technologies and create online leadership identity

1. <u>Managing the technological framework of the network</u>

Staying in our picture of the office building, you can think of setting the framework in two ways, depending on the situation. One way is the design of the office building. A pharmaceutical company decided to connect all floors using a winding staircase along which all coffee and tea kitchens are positioned without doors. When changing floors, it's now easier to pass by people drinking tea and coffee, lowering the threshold to exchange quick pieces of information. The other way, as is true in most cases, involves having to make the best of a given office space. Where is the coffee machine best positioned? What is an appropriate space for a meeting room? etc. These decisions are partly the leader's and partly the group's.

The same applies to setting the framework for global collaboration. You can either start on the level of global IT portfolio management, promoting to introduce new and important tools for collaboration on a global level. One of our customers, Project Global Connect, went down this route after we advised top management on the strategic importance and the current state of global collaboration within the organization as we perceived it.

Or you use the existing portfolio of technological tools and make the best out of it. In this case, the manager needs to decide which tools to should use and push for the necessary process. There are generally two things to consider here:

- Which technologies/tools does the company have that can be used on a global level?; and

- How much media competence do my co-workers and network members have?

Identifying media and their usage for different purposes

Let's have a closer look at the tools.

To set the media framework, answer the following questions.

- Which media exist and are available to every group member?

- Why do group members use specific media and particular features of these (identification of existing competences and good practice)?

- Which media could be used for which purpose?

The second question addresses personal and cultural preferences and experiences and therefore doesn't lend itself to generalization. There is, however, much tested wisdom on choosing the "right" media for the "right" purposes, which we will look at now.

Every communication tool has strengths and weaknesses that vary according to the situation and to user preferences or cultural context. While a medium's strengths are therefore not absolute but always relative, media can be classified in three terms:

- Information richness;

- The number of people that can interact simultaneously (1:1 or 1:n or n:m);

- The time it takes to get a reaction to a contribution: synchronous (interaction partners interact in real time, for example in a chat) or asynchronous communication (reactions are significantly delayed, for example through email).*

Thinking in terms of interactions rather than tools, it is useful to identify the typical interactions that take place in a group. Identifying the type of interaction, its purpose and the setting in which it would "normally" take place in a face-to-face world illuminates what needs to be considered when choosing the corresponding tool or virtual setting.†

Here are some practical examples to illustrate how to simulate reality based on different types of interaction.

Asking quick questions

This type of interaction is usually spontaneous and should be easy to initiate. To allow for quick questions, people typically leave their office doors open to signal approachability. People who work together on the same task often also work together within a short walking distance, or

---

* The following information is taken from Hildebrandt et al. (2013), chapter 8.
† Ibid. for a list of which media to use for which purpose. See also Part IV: "Some concepts from 'Closeness at a Distance'", p. 296.

they always meet at the same table during lunch. This is the "hardware" – the factual – side of this interaction.

There is also a "software" – a behavioural – side. This lies in the implicit agreement that quick questions are questions that can be answered in short time, say two to ten minutes. If people abuse this understanding, knowing that the discussion actually requires thirty minutes to an hour of the other's time and doing this frequently, the openness for quick questions will go down significantly.

These interactions usually take place in a more informal setting and aren't documented in writing.

To ask a quick question online, use IM, chat, SMS or Whatsapp

Mimicking this in the virtual world requires a tool for informal communication that allows signalling, "I am available" or, "Please don't disturb". Instant messenger functions allow the users to see who is currently online and available for a short text-based interaction. A chat room that is open to all group members 24/7 can fulfil the same purpose. In a chat, a question can be addressed to an individual (@Marcus: Do you know…) or to the whole group (@all: Could anyone provide me with…). Another option is using SMS or WhatsApp to send quick questions.

Again, having the tools alone isn't the way to success. It's agreeing on how to use them according to the nature of the interaction and sticking to that agreement that makes them efficient. If this is abused, don't be surprised at being ignored – something that's much easier in virtuality than in person.

Use synchronous and asynchronous media channels to keep in touch online

Maintaining social interaction

Examples of this interaction type include saying "Good Morning", sharing private information, having breakfast together, or sharing a joke or some gossip in the hallway. Social interaction can happen throughout the whole network or on an individual level. On the network level, it requires that all members be enabled and motivated to partake in the interaction. On an individual level, keeping in touch often requires some privacy.

The media used for maintaining social interaction should therefore be 1:1 and n:m tools that can be used synchronously as well as asynchronously. For example, one can react to a chat message immediately (synchronous communication) or later (asynchronous communication). Like for quick questions, IM is a great option to maintain contact on an individual level, while a chat room can be used on a group level. On the group level, video rooms or web-based conferencing systems are great for shared lunches or birthday celebrations online. See Part IV: "Principles of communication and their connection to network and community dynamics", p. 287, for some basic axioms of network communication.

Many of us already use these tools in private life. Just think of how you keep in touch with your friends when you are not able to meet them face-to-face regularly.

Informing

Informing denotes transporting knowledge and information from an individual to a group or to another individual. When informing groups, it's useful to understand the push and pull approach. Pushing information is common in most companies. It means sending out information and trusting that it is noticed. However, in the age of information overload, many people receive so much digital information (mainly via email) that it becomes impossible to read it all. "TMI – too much information" actually results in feeling uninformed. Moreover, a lot of the information isn't even relevant or useful for the receiver, but the sender wanted to make sure to include everyone.

Pushing or pulling information?

The pull approach, on the other hand, is much more efficient. Pulling information means the sender makes it available, while it's the receiver's responsibility to collect those parts that are relevant for them. Many of us use the pull approach in private life. Think of organizing free time activities, for example. We obtain most information about times and locations of games, meetings or trainings from home pages or chat groups.

However, merely storing data in a central place from where it can be pulled may not always suffice in reality. Some level of marketing the data may also be required. In a web conference, for example, data can be marketed by informing participants that a new document has been stored in the shared folder, highlighting why certain aspects could be important information for certain people and addressing them directly.

Delivering personalized and attractive summaries spiced up with some storytelling ensures that information is pulled by the right people.

Deciding

Decision-making requires solid preparation, including stakeholder management and considering cultural aspects. More importantly for the context of this chapter, it also requires discussion and synchronous interactions. Decisions often touch on personal aspects and bring afore differing opinions. It's therefore useful to choose a synchronous communication tool with high media richness and plenty of channels to interact. Allow people to see each other, hear each other, type, see the same documents, draw, vote and so on.

Use web-
conferencing
for virtual
decision-making

Web-based meeting tools like WebEx, Skype for Business (ex-Lync), Adobe Connect, Goto Meeting, SameTime and others are great for this. One of the most important things is to activate webcams so that participants can see each other. Also, the chat function is crucial as it allows quick private exchanges between individual participants as well as questions, observations or feedback with everyone without interrupting the facilitated audio stream.

Note that cultural differences in communication styles can become more pronounced in web conferences. In order to understand the diversity of cultural preferences in a group better, it is helpful to understand how dialogue patterns differ. When one participant in a dialogue is speaking, the other can either interrupt her or wait until she is finished with her statement, then either immediately start speaking or pause before speaking. These three patterns are visualized in the following box.[*]

Cultural differences in communication patterns

Text box 2.1: Communication patterns

Example: Communication and pause patterns

The pattern of dialogues can differ significantly across cultural backgrounds, particularly regarding the pauses made between thoughts or different speakers.

The following three examples of dialogues between persons A and B show different cultural preferences for communication patterns. In an intercultural group, it is essential to understand these cultural differences in order to avoid or overcome frustration and misunderstanding about being interrupted or confronted with silences.

Stop - Start Pattern

Members of cultures that consider time as a primary resource, including Germans or Swiss, tend to dislike pauses and find it difficult to bear them. They usually start speaking the moment the other person stops.

---

* From Hildebrandt et al. (2013), chapter 2.

Stop - Pause Pattern

Members of cultures in which information is collected before taking the initiative and avoiding conflicts is imperative, such as most Asians or some of the Nordic countries, tend to pause between thoughts or speakers. They do that to show that they reflect what's been said and to allow the other to finish their thought. Accepting that pause and being able to bear short periods of silence can be challenging for colleagues from the other cultures.

Talking Over – Stop Pattern

In cultures that value relationships as a primary resource, such as Spain or Brazil, talking over one another is common. Often, people don't wait for a speaker to finish his or her thought. Interruptions are part of the conversational nature. They signal that the one interrupting understood what was said and is now ready to respond. Such a dynamic dialogue is a sign of a good relationship and empathy.

Now imagine a phone conference with members of dialogue cultures 2 and 3, such as a group of Brazilian and Chinese group members. After the conference you might hear the following complaints:

- The Chinese might complain that they had no chance to contribute because the Brazilians kept talking and interrupting each other. "Why did they invite us to the conference at all? They were not interested in our perspective on the issue."

- The Brazilians might complain that the Japanese didn't contribute to the conversation. "There is no point in inviting the Japanese colleagues because they never come up with ideas for problem solving. They always just listen."

What to do? Use the Team Clock.

In diverse groups, phone conferences can be structured with the help of the right tools. Used in agendas, the team clock defines a sequence of speakers that is to be followed throughout the meeting. In a meeting, it reminds partici-pants to address people personally and sequentially, one after the other. In the example of the phone conference between the Brazilian and Japanese colleagues, the team clock is a tool that could be used to facilitate the coexistence of the different communication patterns explained above.

The Team Clock

Figure 2.11: Team Clock

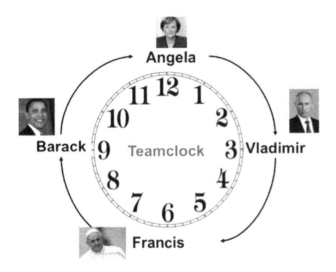

In a call with more than five participants, using a team clock helps to structure members' airtime. Due to the clockwise rotation, they know exactly when they will be asked to speak. We recommend using the team clock three to five times during a session.[*]

_____

*   Ibid.

2. <u>Ensuring that all network members acquire the competences required to perform within this technological framework</u>

To illustrate this point, we will draw on two topics from our book "Closeness at a Distance": media competence and a shared netiquette.* Let's use the office building example again to explain the two concepts.

Media competence is the ability to enter and move around inside an office. Knowing how to actually do the work by finding the meeting room, a colleague's office and the coffee machine. A shared netiquette denotes knowing how to behave in the office. Do we arrive on time, do we say Good Morning to each other, may I take calls during a meeting or even stay away, and should my door remain open?

Media Competence

The level of media competence exposes generational differences like no other. Media competence is about group members' maturity in handling the available technology and dealing with different competence levels within the group. Learning how to use media and communicate virtually is similarly challenging as cultural learning because it requires a will to access and transform deeply held values. An intervention will start by examining whether people have access to the necessary media and the skills to use them.

Don't give up and be stubborn – and do tech checks

The manager's job is to push for developing group members' media competences and for the organization to make the necessary tools available for all. Our recommendation in this context is very simple. Don't give up and be stubborn!

---

* From Hildebrandt et al. (2013), chapter 8.

Members with lower levels of media maturity have to be trained and supported. The leader should connect individually with all members to do so-called tech checks. Tech checks show how savvy someone is allows a quick training on the spot if needed. Often, the typical excuses around avoiding technology are a way to hide people's insecurity in this area.

This is especially important at the beginning of a virtual collaboration when groups and particularly their leaders are often impatient and want things to work immediately. One of the most widespread complaints in this context is about virtual collaboration taking up too much time and being inefficient. However, when thinking about the time used for travelling to face-to-face meetings with a global group, meeting virtually clearly is less time intensive. The difference is simply that the time spent travelling is familiar to people while virtuality often feels alien.

Shared Netiquette

When attending a face-to-face meeting, most people observe certain behavioural norms. In one's culture of origin, one knows where to go, arrives five to ten minutes in advance, and greets those present in the room. If people have to travel to meetings they (the people and the meeting) are usually well prepared with an agenda and presentation slides, for example.

In virtuality, these norms often don't exist and people tend to act less considerately. It can be difficult to develop shared behaviours or a shared netiquette but at the same time, it brings a shared identity. We have observed that a shared netiquette should be negotiated rather than ordered. People need to know and feel that they have a part in creating norms in order to share the responsibility to implement them.

Use the Deep Democracy approach to negotiating a shared netiquette with your network members

Negotiation is a science in and of itself and the virtual leader must master it, just as she needs to be good at facilitation and moderation. Without it, the diversity in a group cannot be included and capitalized on for the purpose of high group performance. When negotiating a shared netiquette with your group, we recommend you do so according to the following six steps that are part of the concept of Deep Democracy.[*]

Steps in Deep Democracy Negotiations
1. **Check: What would you like to improve and why?**
2. **Prepare evaluation: Identify indicators for measuring the improvement of virtual performance**
3. **Reflect: How would you bring the topic(s) into the group?**
4. **Facilitate a process according to the following success factors:**
   - **Collect all views/identify all involved interests, good practice, or wishes**
   - **Hunt for the No/the alternative views by identifying weak signals/areas of disagreement**
   - **Spread the No/the alternative view/the weak signal and add minority wisdom**
   - **Say sorry if it is not possible to fulfil the needs/ask, "What do you need?"**
5. **Plan in advance: How would you keep the topic(s) alive?**
6. **Use indicators transparently: How would you monitor the topic(s)?**

3. Role modelling efficient virtual interaction: Building online leadership presence

The network leader must ask himself two central questions.

Are you available to your network and do your network members know how and when to reach you online?

- Am I available to my network (time and place)?

- Do I come across as a human being and as a leader online (online identity)?

Please take a moment and ask yourself if you are available

---

[*] See Hildebrandt et al. (2013), chapter 7, for detailed guidance on this process. See also Mindell and Lewis.

to your network and if your network members know how and when to reach you online. We know they can send you an email, but these are often rather impersonal interactions and not all cultures, especially those which are strongly relationship oriented, really like this.

A good way of being present is establishing virtual office hours. It could be every Tuesday between 10 am and 12 pm that your "door is open". Here we recommend a tool with a camera so group members have the possibility to see you and talk about topics they have on their agenda, both personal and work-related topics. It is important that this is not an appointment one has to schedule or book in advance. This way, people can feel that a manager is present and that they can reach out for him.

Establish regular virtual office hours

Another way of signalling your availability is using the green, orange and red lights of your instant messaging system (IM). This allows your people to see whether you are in or out of the virtual office, occupied or available for a short interaction. See Part IV: "Principles of communication and their connection to network and community dynamics", p. 289, for some basic axioms of network communication.

Signal your availability

Online identity

Now ask yourself if your network members perceive you as a human being when interacting with you virtually. This is a question about your online identity. Speaking of it, when did you last look yourself up on Google? Did an authentic photograph of you come up?

Online leadership identity is about how other people "see" you online. Do others feel that they are interacting with a person and does that impression conform to who you are as a leader/colleague? Think about yourself for a moment and how you behave when you interact online. Take a look

How do you come across online?

at your emails, reflect on your last call or web meeting. Was that "Online You" the same as the "You" in a face-to-face meeting?

To understand the concept of online (leadership) identity better it is helpful to examine what makes a person come across as a person in the virtual, and especially in the text-based, world. To that end, we would like to suggest three dimensions of online presence. The right mix that lets you and your leadership brand (see chapter "Leadership branding", p. 65) come across authentically enables others to perceive you as a "real" person online.

The three dimensions of a person's online identity are the three types of virtual presence: cognitive presence[*], social presence[†] and leadership presence[‡] (see Part IV: "Some concepts from 'Closeness at a Distance'", p. 296).

Cognitive presence

Cognitive
presence

Cognitive presence is the extent to which people are able to construct meaning and knowledge in the framework of a process of reflection and communication (in a virtual room). Cognitive presence can be illustrated by associating it with the head of the manager. The circle represents the head = cognitive presence.

Figure 2.12: Cognitive presence

---

*   Garrison, Anderson, Archer (2000).
†   Pächter, Schweizer, Weidemann (2002).
‡   Garrison, Anderson, Archer (2000).

Cognitive presence stands for task and data orientation. To spot unique signs of cognitive presence in the virtual communication of a person, look out for cues that give clear answers to the following questions:

- What has to be done at what time? Which action items are prescribed?

- Is there important information or knowledge transferred in the message?

- Does the message include any plans or checkpoints?

- Are there any "how to…" descriptions?

- Etc…

Social presence

Social presence is defined by the degree to which the partner of interaction is perceived as a person/human being (in a virtual room). While cognitive presence gives food for thought, social presence is more about emotions. The heart symbolizes this dimension of online identity.

Social presence

Figure 2.13: Social presence

Social presence lends the human touch to communication processes. Typical cues for this type of online presence include:

- Saying "Good Morning" online using an emoticon such as the coffee icon or a smiley.

- Including social information in virtual meetings, for example by sharing the gossip of the week at the beginning of a meeting; playing small games such as using web-based software to create a team rhythm simultaneously; or celebrating a birthday where someone in one location plays the guitar and colleagues in other locations sing and local co-workers present the cake; etc.

- Sharing information from one's private life.

- Spending time online with group members without an agenda or topics to work on. A Friday afternoon coffee chat could be an example for this.

Leadership presence

Leadership
presence

Leadership Presence is defined as the design, moderation and organization of cognitive and social processes (in virtual rooms) with the purpose of achieving results. Leadership is about moving people towards shared objectives or in the direction of a fixed strategy. The legs of the manager symbolize leadership presence.

Figure 2.14: Leadership presence

Speaking of motivation, providing orientation or setting the framework in which the network can cooperate are signs of leadership presence in the communication of a person. They can include:

- Pushing IT to provide everybody with access to the necessary technologies, and, based on this,

- Providing what is necessary in terms of technology to enable the network to have a virtual team coffee

- Training everyone's media competences accordingly

- Creating a healthy rhythm and sequence for the web meetings*

- Establishing online availability time (virtual office hours)

- Conducting critical incident sessions (see chapter "Shaping global dialogue", p. 159).

Stephen Karnik (see his interview on p. 222) describes nicely how he offers "conscious time" every week to his colleagues across the globe to be available to them to discuss issues and concerns and answer questions. He calls weekly web-conferences and tailors his schedule to accommodate the different time zones.

When the three dimensions of online presence come together in the way a person communicates virtually, a holistic impression of that person's online identity with all its human facets is created and symbolized by the following image.

Figure 2.15: Online presence

To make a positive impact on your communication partners in a virtual collaboration space, it is crucial to be

---

* See Hildebrandt et al. (2013), chapter 8, for the concept of the heartbeat of a virtual group.

perceived as an authentic human being. If you are not perceived as that – because, for example, people can't distinguish your email from an email created by an automatic email notification system – you might run into problems. In virtuality, it's much easier than in co-location for others to ignore you, delete your messages or, as we say, to "life hack" you. For everyday people make a decision about to whom they will give their time and energy and provide their services, and who won't receive this attention. Most people's to-do lists exceed their time. Priority setting is therefore key to a productive work life. So you are less likely to be ignored by someone online and more likely to be included in their list of priorities when they feel that they know and feel (virtually) close to you.

Think of it in terms of this scenario. You are driving your car in the middle of a traffic jam. The two-lane street merges into one lane. Another driver signals to change lanes in front of you. If you don't want to let them in you'll probably try to ignore them because once you've established eye contact, it becomes difficult to pretend they aren't there. Once you have looked at each other, you are likely to feel obligated to let the other pass. They have become a person with a face.

Similarly, if a person's online identity lacks in one of the parts or is strongly imbalanced, the following extreme types of online identity may appear.

Figure 2.16: The Brain, The Action Man, The Open Heart and The Invisible.

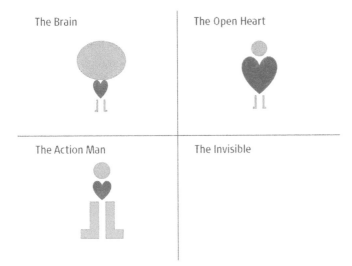

The Brain

The Brain is demanding, always wanting something from others. They hardly share any personal topics and tend to communicate only through email. The content of the communication is mainly fact driven. In consequence, the Brain can come across as very impersonal, seemingly taking no interest in others and perceiving them merely as an instrument to fulfil a task.

The Action Man

The Action Man tends to bring too much structure and rigidity to communication. They often have intense discussions about goals and plans on too high or abstract of a (company) level. Why are we doing this? How does this fit with the company strategy? etc. At the same time, they like organizing and coordinating others. They can therefore come across as a bit too "bossy".

The Open Heart

The Open Heart shares a lot of private information and often prefers phone and video to email communication. They tend to start communication with personal questions and show more emotions in the process. In text-based correspondence they like to use emoticons. As a result, they can come across as lacking focus and may acquire a reputation of spending too much time on "nothing".

The Invisible

People often don't notice the Invisible's existence due to her or his minimal interaction. They remain mostly silent during calls and discussions. Others can forget to inform or invite them to meetings.

In order to avoid any of these caricatured online identities and to come across as a balanced human being in virtual interaction, it's important to remain authentic and real, just the way you are in person. To reflect your online identity, it's useful to analyze your email and other text-based communication and compare it with how you would have communicated the same message in a face-to-face situation. We recommend combining this reflection with your work on creating a leadership branding (see chapter "Leadership branding", p. 65) that is visible online.

Exercises

Exercise 1: Interpreting an intercultural chat protocol

Read through the real-life chat protocol from two colleagues below. Then:

1. Identify signs of social, cognitive and leadership presence.

2. Do you think the October 7th deadline will be met? How could the response (16:21) "perfect! :)" be interpreted in this context? Was there enough leadership presence to achieve this commitment?

3. In your opinion, what did the Brazilian colleague expect when asking the German co-worker about the responsible person in a certain office (16:27)? Was the expectation met and how could the response (16:28) "ok.... I'll check it!" be interpreted in this context?

Brasilien(16:15)	Hello Deutschland
Deutschland (16:16)	Hello Brazil, how are you? ha!
Brasilien(16:16)	I'm just fine and you?
Deutschland(16:17)	Me, too.
Brasilien(16:17)	I still have to check for you the x texts...
Brasilien(16:17)	Things are very busy around here.... today my day is a bit better I'll take a look at it.
Brasilien(16:18)	OK?
Deutschland(16:20)	Yes, absolutely ok! You can send them piece by piece – is that suitable?
Brasilien(16:20)	sure!
Brasilien(16:20)	thanks a lot for your understanding...
Deutschland(16:21)	Ok, fine. However, the final deadline must be 7th of October.
Brasilien(16:21)	perfect! :)
Deutschland(16:22)	well then, have a good day and soon a wonderful week-end!
Brasilien(16:22)	another thing... is your department responsible for the application X?
Deutschland(16:24)	No, we aren't. This is Mr. A's one. Please contact A B.
Brasilien(16:25)	I'm checking if this is the right name of the application...

Brasilien(16:25)	just a sec..
Brasilien(16:26)	X Management, is that X, right?
Brasilien(16:26)	in the past Z gave me some infor- mation about it
Deutschland(16:26)	Yes, it is.
Deutschland(16:27)	Yes, but nor she neither our department is responsible any more. Or do you need access via the C Portal? We still have a team here.
Brasilien(16:27)	do you know who in Mr. A office is responsible for it?
Deutschland(16:28)	I think it's A B.
Deutschland(16:28)	At least someone in his team.
Brasilien(16:28)	ok.... I'll check it!
Brasilien(16:29)	thank you very much!
Deutschland(16:29)	You are welcome. See you!
Brasilien(16:29)	:)

Exercise 2: Check your organization's media tools

1. Contact your IT department or someone who is in charge of collaboration tools at your organization. Identify which tools are available and understand which ones can be used locally and which ones globally.

2. Invest some time to understand the tools.

3. Compare the local and global tools with regard to your local group and global network members. Who has access to what? What can be improved and how?

Exercise 3: List global network interactions

1. Together with your network, develop a list of all the interactions that exist or should exist among the global network (asking questions, brainstorming, making decisions, keeping in contact and so on).

2. Together, brainstorm which media tools are best suited for these communication purposes. Identify personal preferences and experiences among members. Be sensitive to the differing cultural preferences.

Exercise 4: Evaluate media competences online

1. Schedule a virtual session with each of your group members that is rich in media functions (voice + video + document sharing).

2. Dedicate the session to evaluating the media competence of each member.

Exercise 5: Who are you online?

Think of how others perceive you when meeting you face-to-face. Maybe you could ask others how they perceive you when interacting with you.

Then compare that with how you behave when you interact online. Is that the same person?

Exercise 6: Reflecting your online behaviour

Reflect on your online behaviours when connecting with others, using the following questions.

1. How often do you call your colleagues? Do you prefer email to phone calls?

2. How active were you in your last online meeting? Thinking of the elements of your online identity (cognitive, social and leadership presence), how did each of them fare?

3. How often do you connect with other network members to maintain a social connection?

Exercise 7: Online identity in emails
1. Read through some of your emails.

2. Analyze the sentences to identify social presence, cognitive presence and leadership presence.

3. How might others perceive your online identity?

Summary

One of the central leadership responsibilities in network organizations is enabling collaboration across the network through the efficient and tailored use of technology. Mastering collaboration tools is essential for establishing an attractive virtual office space where network members enjoy performing. Another central element is creating online identity on the part of the leader and his group members through cultivating a balance of cognitive, social and leadership presence when interacting virtually.

Shaping global dialogue

Interview with Chunhu Wang

Director of Global Integration

Figure 2.17: Chunhu Wang's complexity image

Here is what Chunhu Wang says about his choice of an image that depicts the complexity he moves through:

"All complexity has its source in the interplay of Yin and Yang and is therefore also not complex at all. This means for me if I tackle complex issues I try to think and act as simply as possible."

Profile
- ❖ Director of Global Integration, working from the German site
- ❖ Chinese, with German citizenship
- ❖ 50 years old
- ❖ Married, two children
- ❖ Responsible for corporate and business culture integration

Chunhu gained a degree in Journalism at Fudan University in Shanghai and Public Communication at Free University of Berlin, and also studied management theory and sociology. Before starting his current position in April/ May 2015, he was responsible for business development in China at Bertelsmann and held several positions as interface manager of Chinese-German locations at two Chinese companies. At one of them, he was also Director of HR as well as Personal Assistant of the Chairman at the Chinese headquarters.

The complexity wherein Chunhu operates

As an experienced manager of Chinese-German corporate interfaces, Chunhu is very experienced with navigating complexity arising from the mix of organizational challenges and cultural differences. "The complexity is that you have managers from different countries at first level, so they have a different cultural background. Secondly, you have Chinese managers who are totally different from each other in their Chinese contexts. In China we have state-owned companies and private companies. Private companies, for example many high-tech companies, tend to be very westernized. And some industrial companies – like in the automotive industry, heavy machinery industry or coal industry – are typically "Chinese Style". It affects the communication with the Western managers, they tend to have a lot of problems. So in this case you need someone, who should not only have the ability to translate one language into another, but also someone who can translate something between the lines. The cultural factors bring in a lot of complexity but the specific character of a person makes things even more complicated. For example, one of my current Chinese management partners is someone who says something and then you have to guess what is behind it. Even among Chinese he has been identified as someone who communicates very, very indirectly with people. So altogether I would say the cultural differences and the character differences combined make my job very difficult."

Chunhu goes on to assess the proportions of family, matrix and network parts of his organization. About the family portion he says, "I would say for the companies I worked for at top-management level it is more like a family structure. If two top-managers, even their subordinates or two department leaders, cannot solve a problem between these two departments or between these two top-managers, they just go to the boss. The boss goes to the chairman for a judgment.

This leads him to the matrix portion of his work. "We also try to build up the standard process according to which the operation will be running automatically. The problem is we are not experiencing the standards, the systems are not the same in these locations as those in the other locations. Even after a merger or an acquisition we have totally different systems – management systems and even IT infrastructures. So we haven't spent a lot of time in the past two or three years to start this standardization process, which we are now going to change. So I would say, the second type, the "machine" which you have mentioned, actually targets the goal we are now striving for. This is also why I am taking over this position especially created for me: Director of Global Integration."

Regarding the network, Chunhu explains, "I already had some personal relationship with my German colleagues while I was not in Germany. They were happy to finally have someone at headquarters who speaks German. They are willing to speak to you even if they have nothing to do with you, because they are not from the HR department, they are discussing an issue with you irrelevant to HR, but to business development or to research and development. They want to talk to you: 'Chunhu, can you please explain this to my colleagues in your IT department?' So we have a telephone conference together and they would like that I translate for them. Even though they have their own interpreters on both sides, but in this case I think I got the trust. Irrespective of the kind of province they come from, they want to have you as the first contact person. This is networking somehow. If we have some colleagues in our headquarters with a background in Western countries or that speak foreign languages and know Western business styles, those also have the same experience as I do. They will be approached in many ways, even if the issues touched upon have nothing to do with their work."

Chunhu's strategies to reduce and navigate this complexity: What has worked and what hasn't worked so well, and why?

In Chunhu's context as a global leader, reducing complexity especially applies to the communication between the Chinese and the German corporate sites. "When talking about virtual communication you include various communication instruments, like telephone, videoconference, telephone conference, email or other platforms for online communication. But in my company in China, I mostly use the phone conference or the individual phone. I chat with my colleagues in the daughter companies. We seldom use videoconference. Usually I like to first know the people personally before I use the telephone as a virtual instrument to communicate with them. We have yearly or sometimes quarterly meetings with HR managers in the daughter companies. At the very beginning I used this platform to know each of our HR managers, of each company, and then I often used the telephone as well as email to connect with them."

Interestingly, Chunhu doesn't find it more challenging to manage relationships over a distance within China rather than face-to-face because, "I know all of them. I have put emphasis on knowing them personally. The first thing I did when I started my job in the headquarters in China was to visit each local company in other provinces beyond Shanghai. I let them show me around the company as well as informing me about the HR activities in each company, so actually I know very well what they are doing and what kind of challenges they have. With this background I didn't have any problem with directing their daily and strategic work through virtual communication."

However, it becomes a different story on an international level. Chunhu says, "This is really a big challenge. Our German location is our biggest daughter abroad so I also paid them a visit. I got to know our HR colleague there, so we can communicate well with each other, especially as I speak German, so there are some personal relationships. I know what they are talking about and I understand what kind of problems they have in the interaction with the headquarters. They feel very comfortable with someone at headquarters who understands their mentality, so every time when they have a problem they just call me directly and say: 'Chunhu, I have this situation. Could you please help me to clarify it to our colleagues in the headquarters?' In this case I am also able to help them, to clarify the situation and to clarify what led to this situation, so that people can easily find a common solution. But in America, in the Czech Republic and in Romania, we have other problems, because we do not know them very well personally. We have never seen each other before. And headquarters also has the policy to say: Let the local managers solve their own problems. This is somewhat okay, it is good but it is also not good, because they do not emphasize any individual or personal interaction with the local manager anymore. In some way I would say we neglect the business build-up."

Here, reducing complexity is a bigger challenge. "Of course I plan to do something about that, but the problem is: If the top-management of the whole group is not realizing how important the interaction is at personal level with colleagues in foreign countries, then you do not get enough resources to do that. For example, to organize an actual visit at the departmental level, to have our colleagues in the HR department from America or from European countries visit us and vice versa. Some are saying: HR is a matter of top management and I understand that much better than before since I joined these two Chinese companies."

Chunhu's reactions to the central parameters of leading in the face of hyper-complexity

- <u>Shaping and influencing organizational communities</u> – Yes. We are going to start an integration process and I am taking over this position. That would be a focal point for me in the future, but not right now.

- <u>Creating virtual closeness and global collaboration spaces</u> – Yes

- <u>Framework setting and mastering technology</u> – Yes

- <u>Dealing with complexity</u> – Yes

- <u>Personal branding</u> – Yes

- <u>Contextual leadership</u> – Yes

- <u>Creating a culture of voicing</u> – Yes, this is a point I stress everywhere. Communication without feedback is no communication for me. I think everybody knows the importance of feedback, but in reality you don't find it a lot. It has something to do with the unclear efficiency of work and responsibilities. If the Chinese do not feel that they are responsible for something, they don't give it.

- <u>Measuring success</u> – Yes. Success must be measurable otherwise it will be difficult. And success is always linked to some practical bonus and also some oral compliments. You have to give some reasons for these compliments, give some reasons for these bonuses. So it should be measurable.

Shaping global dialogue

"No news is good news." This phrase has a long tradition in some Western cultures. It basically expresses trust in the other party of a collaborative setting on two levels. First, we trust that the partner has the means to achieve the joint goal and we need not follow up daily on the work process. Second, we believe that if something is going wrong our work partner will take the initiative to inform us about it.

No news is bad news

In the global context, however, this may no longer be true. Due to cultural reasons our cooperation partners might:

- not inform us about any problems on their side as this could lead to the risk of losing face, or

- believe that the task to be performed is not important as it is not being followed-up daily, or

- inform us about problems in such an implicit way that we can't decode the message from a cultural perspective that values more direct communication.

On the other hand there might be technical reasons. The other may be ill and therefore offline or may even have left the company. The latter is quite likely in countries with high levels of staff fluctuation.

Therefore, we should rather say, "No news is bad news." Against this background, we believe that two of the main leadership tasks include

- creating a framework that allows for a continuous stream of relevant information between all network members, and

- promoting a communication culture in which critical aspects of global cooperation (as well as appreciation) can and will be addressed.

We call the latter "voicing culture".

Chunhu Wang is a good example of a leader who understands the crucial importance of building and maintaining a voicing culture in global business environments. As a leader whose job it is to facilitate and translate between the German and Chinese and many other cultures, he knows the intricacies and challenges of creating continuous dialogue to increase clarity and efficiency. For Chunhu, communication only becomes real and efficient communication when feedback is practised consistently. He therefore works to be in dialogue with his people all the time.

While the aforementioned reasons for prioritizing communication should be convincing enough, there are further aspects of communication related especially to the network aspects of hyper-complex environments that merit examination. In the following section, we will focus on these aspects and offer practical answers to the challenges discussed above.

What are the special aspects of communication within network contexts?

- In order to be able to shape successful leadership initiatives it is very important to have enough context knowledge and data or contextual intelligence (see chapter "Contextual leadership", p. 93) in order to recognize weak signals or patterns that help us to understand the dynamics of the organization.

- On the other hand, we introduced the example of the paramecium (p. 33) to show that acts of communication help us to "stir up the organization" and thus probe the environment: Is there any resonance within the organization to the ideas or initiatives I as a leader would like to pursue? The leadership aspect of this is called personal branding (see chapter "Leadership branding", p. 65).

- And finally, especially for generation Y (see Part IV: "Some remarks about Generation Y", p. 277), it is very important to stabilize the network by creating a sense of belonging for people who are distributed internationally and have little face-to-face interaction.

All these facets of communication within networks have one common denominator. Attractiveness is the key principle that determines the dynamics of networks. But in most cases, attractive "poles" meet with resistance. If there is light there is also shadow, and any new initiative will be challenged by people who are critical about it.

However, if you don't achieve a high intensity of discussion and feedback – positive as well as negative – around your leadership initiative, it is unlikely to be successful. In the long run, this polarity should be overcome in the same way dilemmas can be resolved on a higher level of perception, hierarchy or organizational structure, for example (see also chapter "Influencing the organization", p. 194).

For a more abstract analysis of the interplay between communication and network dynamics as well as the concept of virtual closeness, see Part IV: "The concepts of groups, networks and communities", p. 269, "Principles of communication and their connection to network and community dynamics", p. 287, for some basic axioms of network communication, and "Some concepts from 'Closeness at a Distance'", p. 296.

In this chapter we focus on the first aspect that consists of two core questions. First, how can a global exchange of information be stimulated? And second, how can a culture be created that allows people to continuously communicate their context and openly address their perceptions and feelings concerning possible business opportunities as well as the current state of cooperation within their virtual group and existing leadership initiatives?

We call this culture a "responding" or "voicing" culture where people continuously and transparently respond to signals from their work environment. An important element of this voicing culture is the well-known concept of feedback culture. How these two special elements of communication – **voicing** and **feedback** – can be developed professionally will be shown in the following.

Javier Escobedo (see his interview on p. 253) confirms the importance of building a culture of voicing and feedback when he says, "This is super, super important. Easier said than done. There are some places where it will just not happen and you will just have to get rid of the people that do not have the tendency to provide standard feedback. And there is the opposite of that. You would think the opposite of giving feedback is giving no feedback, but for me the opposite of giving feedback is talking behind people's backs. That is the opposite, because no feedback is just zero. So if feedback is one, no feedback is zero. But minus one is just talking – not talking directly about things. As much as I think feedback is important, when there is a backchannel communication and things do not get communicated in the right way in the right place because there is no openness for whatever reason, that minus one will kill you. You will start losing people. So that is a big issue."

Developing a voicing culture and a feedback culture

Let us start by defining the differences and similarities of these two acts of communication.

Voicing

We define voicing as follows:

- Voicing is sharing with others (verbally, non-verbally, para-verbally, text- or object- based, face-to-face or mediated by technology) an observation, a personal behaviour, a feeling and/or an internal state of being.

  Voicing defined

- The triggers that lead to the act of voicing can be external (e.g. observed behaviours from network members) or internal (e.g. an inner feeling), tangible (e.g. a product that I have in my hand) or abstract (e.g. a mental model).

- The purpose of voicing is mainly to provide contextual cues for others that help others to better understand the sender's behaviour.

Over the years we have learned that feedback is essential in the professional context. Our attitude towards voicing is different. Most of us are not used to communicating to others continuously and proactively what we are doing, what we are experiencing and what we are thinking or feeling. We have to overcome the common attitude, "Out of sight, out of mind", and create virtual closeness* (see Part IV: "Some concepts from 'Closeness at a Distance'", p. 296) by keeping the other network members in the loop about our local context to enable them to see the bigger picture of international cooperation. This is the principal

---

* Hildebrandt et al. (2013), chapter 1.

The Avoidance-
Barometer: 9
steps of not
communicating

basis for anticipating critical situations and supporting each other in these moments. This makes cooperation a little more predictable and is the means for creating fast and flexible cooperation processes.

The importance of good communication between the members of an international network is non-negotiable. If a significant bond is not built amongst all in the group, relations will go quickly from bad to worse. Based on Myrna Lewis' Avoidance-Barometer, feelings of disconnect will eventually progress to complete avoidance. Her theory recognizes nine escalating stages in which these disconnected team members increase distance between themselves and the project. She suggests that this process begins with jokes and sarcasm: seemingly unthreatening. These evolve to excuses as to why tasks are incomplete or why the team member missed a meeting. This attitude makes it clear that the individual does not regard the goals of the project of high importance. From this point on, things get uglier.

The next symptoms of avoidance to surface are gossip, refusal to adequately communicate, and insulting commentary. The work is then severely affected because the person has now lost respect for the collaboration or project. As a result, the performance level sinks constantly, leading to work stoppage and finally complete withdrawal from the project. The damage done by such a group member can be tragic for the project as it relies on its workers to fulfil their duties and responsibilities so that it may meet its deadlines. Introducing the team to the Avoidance-Barometer before major problems materialize may give the group members a chance to reflect on their behaviour and recognize their faults. From there they can work to solve the minor issues before the project loses its members and its efficiency.

Figure 2.18: Avoidance-Barometer

Feedback

Feedback fits in the definition of voicing as a special case.

- Feedback is a form of voicing triggered by others' behaviour.

- The purpose of feedback is to communicate the impact of the observed behaviour and the corresponding need for the behaviour to either stop, continue or start to change (increase/decrease).

Feedback defined

Stefan Meister and Marcus Hildebrandt have introduced feedback resonance as a quality criterion for feedback that takes the impact of feedback on the person and their context into account. Feedback should be resonant.

This fits well with the concept of networks and their underlying dynamics.

- It is based on the concept, "Communication is the response you get"*, and

- It takes the reverse perspective – the shift form push to pull in networks – into account. Arnulf Keese confirmed this in his interview by saying, "You have to earn your feedback" (p. 94).

---

* Honor Cooper Kovacz, private correspondence with Marcus Hildebrandt, 1999.

Resonant
feedback

Resonant Feedback

Feedback is resonant when one or more of the following quality criteria can be observed.

- Reciprocity: the feedback process had an impact on the behaviours of all communication partners.

- (Virtual) Closeness: all communication partners feel that the closeness between them or to the organization or process has increased.

- Shared added value: after one or more feedback loops all communication partners are convinced that this feedback process has added value.

In that way, resonant feedback increases the attractiveness of the feedback process for all participants. This, in turn, increases the probability of people giving or receiving feedback and of a positive impact on the context.

In the following, we will look at how to develop a voicing and a feedback culture.

Establishing a voicing culture

From the multitude of workshops we have facilitated with the objective of improving virtual and face-to-face meetings in international contexts, we have collected the following approaches to creating a voicing culture[*].

Specific steps
recommended
for creating a
voicing culture

- Establish a biweekly Jour Fixe that is held on the same day and at the same hour for having a 1:1 conversation with one of your co-workers. Talk about professional as well as personal topics. Manage expectations, praise and criticize. These meetings should have a visible impact on the collaboration.

---

[*] See Jehle (2015).

- Establish a transparent and official escalation process. This is especially needed in matrix organizational environments.

- Introduce fixed availability times during which your co-workers can reach you.

- Allocate time slots in meetings to discuss lessons learned and evaluate both the results quality as well as the process quality of your collaboration.

- Jointly define and create shared behaviours that promote voicing.

- Establish an atmosphere of trust and create a learning culture that allows mistakes to be seen as an opportunity for all to learn.

- Facilitate meetings so that all perspectives and voices are heard. Address all participants personally in an appreciative way.

- Practice clear expectation management. What kind of voicing (proactive communication) is needed? How will you ensure voicing has an impact so that people see a benefit to doing it?

- When discussing critical incidents, rather than assigning blame, treat the past as a "black box" to identify future solutions. What's gone is gone. What can we do in order to prevent this from happening in the future?

- Create voicing tandems. Share your need to voice with a colleague and then voice jointly.

- Share your experiences in tandems or groups of three. When was it difficult for you to voice something? What was hindering you? What could have helped you to voice? Then collect ideas to promote voicing in your network based on these experiences.

- Establish ways to voice anonymously. For a web

conference, create a PowerPoint slide for rating team performance and ask team members to give their ratings using the anonymous annotation function of the conferencing tool or use any anonymous voting system.

A more structured approach to building a voicing culture is the Critical Incidents method [*].

The Critical Incidents Method

The Critical Incidents Method: A structured approach to building a voicing culture

As managers begin to expand from solely local business to involvement in international projects, they suddenly realize that the staff meetings they would normally call on short notice are no longer a viable option for dealing with problems in their widely spread networks. When scheduled video calls become the most intimate communication setting for a business group, it stands to reason that the communication techniques of a traditional office must change to fit the unique demands of a virtual group.

The critical incidents technique[†] tackles many hurdles that international project networks (with teams at the very heart of the network) must take and proves to be an ideal way to establish lively, productive dialogue as a global network's healthy habit.

Critical incidents are typically challenges but can also be successes

The critical incidents technique provides a structured dialogue format which is designed as a check-in for the network members, so that topics of confusion or concern can be effectively analyzed and the group can reach a joint solution. The members are in rotation, so that each time that the group or part of the network (e.g. core team) meets for a critical incidents meeting a new person gets to pick a critical incident which concerns all members.

---

[*]   Ibid.

[†]   Flanagan (1954).

During the conversation it is also useful to discuss the victories of the group, if even only small ones.

Mentioning concerns and failures will keep critical incidents meetings from becoming a dreaded business requirement. Reporting that a group member completed a set of tasks in record time despite little forewarning, or thanking a network member for taking on extra work to help another member with the overwhelming workload, are common examples of positive comments which should be brought up at a critical incidents meeting. While discussing the positives at each meeting can be a wonderful addition to the conversation, the focus of most critical incidents meetings is, logically, the critical incident. Typical topics up for discussion are the tardiness or inadequacy of requested information, confusion with whose job is whose, major project or process failures, events leading to customer dissatisfaction or just how to signal to the others when something needs urgent action.

Structuring a critical incidents session

Due to the critical incidents technique's unnatural structure for communication – there is first a strong focus on the context before one tries to find solutions – it may be difficult for team members, especially those who want to find immediate answers, to abide by the setup of the meeting. Since the leader needs to participate in all meetings, it is helpful to invite a separate, neutral party to regulate the conversation and keep it within the structure of the critical incidents technique. This moderator will have several functions in the meeting. For the sake of his assisting capabilities, the moderator should thoroughly understand the communication tool should there be a need for technical clarification, and also have a high proficiency of global English or any other language agreed upon to support those in the group who get hung up on the spoken language.

How to structure critical incidents sessions: Moderating is key

In these cases, it may be that the moderator types in dictation so that all can follow along. Foremost, moderators need to have a substantial social competence. They are responsible for creating a safe space where the global team feels safe to speak in full confidence. This space becomes the closest thing to a shared office that this virtual network will get, so they must treat it as such. Values and rules will be made clear in the first meetings, so that the ground rules are laid out and all are aware of what is expected. This experienced moderator may stick with the group until the end of its project, but once it finds a rhythm in the critical incidents technique, the network members can choose to take turns carrying out the duty of the moderator.

Frequency of synchronous meetings and technology

Knowing that the heartbeat* – the frequency of synchronous meetings – has to be regular in order to increase performance it becomes the responsibility of the leader to make the critical incidents meetings happen regularly in a format where all members feel comfortable and can communicate clearly. In order to create some routine, the leader should invite the entire group or the core team to regularly scheduled meetings, for example once every three weeks. It is one of the leader's tasks to pick a tool of communication which satisfies the needs of the global network. The most suitable tools are those which appeal to the most senses in order to best replace the face-to-face communication. Tools like WebEx, Skype for Business (ex Lync), Google Hangout and Adobe Connect have a combination of written, video and voice communication and are also well suited for international communication. However, a tool is completely useless if its functions are foreign to the network members. In some cases, it may be necessary for the leader to conduct an instructional and trouble-shooting meeting with the members until all are familiar with the functions of the project leader's chosen

---

*   Hildebrandt et al. (2013), chapter 8.

tool (see chapter "Mastering technologies and creating online leadership identity", p. 122).

Once the group understands how to use the tool, the critical incidents meetings should all have the same agenda and flow.

Meeting design

Starting the meeting, breaking the ice

To start, the moderator will welcome all participants and as a group they will spend ten to fifteen minutes answering a quick question presented by the moderator – a kind of ice-breaker or check-in. This part of the meeting is not specific to the critical incident set aside for the meeting. While the starting phase of the meeting is not necessarily formal, it is important that all members are fully dedicated to the conversation, because the mood of the introduction flows into the remaining sections of the meeting.

Round 1: Explaining the subject and asking questions – 20-30 minutes

After the warm-up, the person in charge of the meeting´s critical incident has five minutes to explain the subject. Directly following the description is a round of questions to clarify the details of the critical-incident in an effort to understand the situation fully. During these twenty to thirty minutes only questions may be asked –suggestions for solutions will come in a later phase of the meeting. Questions hinting at solutions like, "Did you try xy...?" should be avoided. Better questions are: Who was involved? What did you do? What were the reactions? What was the sequence of events? etc. By discouraging problem solving in this round, it challenges each individual to think further into the topic and to listen to the others' questions. This round reinforces a deep understanding for the issue and the chance to consider others'

confusions. Moderators must be sure that every participant provides input in this round. This rule is put in place
to ensure that all are actively present in the discussion
and, because of the limited time, that all get a chance
to ask their questions. Sometimes this means that the
moderator, often supplementing their authoritative statements with a running timer, will have to remind the
verbose members to respect their time limit and keep
their speeches concise.

Figure 2.19: Team clock

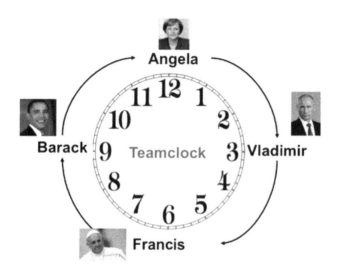

(See also chapter "Mastering technologies and creating
online leadership identity", p. 122)

The team clock is a useful tool to sequence contributions[*]. Not only does it give a sequence of who should
speak when, but it also represents how the time in each
phase of the meeting must be split evenly amongst the
members. It also keeps all the other members alert and
on task because they know that they, too, will have to
contribute. Getting a few emails answered during these

---

* Ibid.

meetings is not usually worth the embarrassment that would come from being caught off-task.

Round 2: Sharing perspectives – 10-15 minutes

Still in the team clock format, members share their thoughts, opinions, viewpoints and observations regarding the critical incident during their turn in the perspective round. This session should last ten to fifteen minutes, but one should note that this time is still not meant to search for a solution.

Round 3: Identifying solutions – 20-30 minutes

A solution is then sought in the next, appropriately named, solution round. The goal in these twenty to thirty minutes is to come to a conclusion that suits all. In this time, the group should also pinpoint the source of the critical incident, so that they may avoid the hassle of revisiting the issue in the future. Although the moderator may minute the meeting and send the information to the project members, a critical incidents meeting does not force the partakers to abide by any solutions found in the meeting. The meeting's goal is to achieve group under-standing through stimulating communication rather than to enforce new regulation to optimize efficiency. More or less, the notes are a collection of suggestions for positive change.

Round 4: Feedback

At the end of the meeting, each member should give feedback to the group. They can voice what they liked about the meeting, what could have been better, or which everyday lesson they will take away from it. After all have made their last statements, the moderator will conclude the meeting.

8 participants
are ideal

The number of partakers in a critical incident meeting makes a difference, because of the time limit provided by the team clock in conjunction with the critical incidents technique. It is suggested that the ideal number of participants is eight. If the global network has more members, then a rotation schedule can be set up – at least one person from each location should be present at any given meeting.

Rotating
meeting times
to accommodate
different time
zones

While the meetings should be scheduled on a specific day of the week (e.g. Tuesday), in consideration for the varying time zones, the time of day at which the meeting takes place should be switched frequently. As a consequence of this, the same people need not always attend the meetings very late or very early in their day. Volunteering to share the burden of inconvenient time slots is a sign of respect for the sacrifices of the other co-workers and it creates a sense of belonging and gratitude.

It is true that this culture of virtual communication deviates from the natural understanding of speech and interaction. However, mastering this form of communication is absolutely crucial for success in intercultural communication for international networks. Though there are too many situation-dependent factors to give an absolute formula as to how one should learn to communicate virtually, using methods like the team clock and critical incidents techniques does well to make this form of communication manageable. With a little patience and foresight, these methods will encourage productive communication in a network spread out around the globe, allowing it to come together and work effectively.

Establishing a feedback culture

Feedback is
culture sensitive

Based on the axioms of human communication in Western countries has evolved a feedback culture that can be described with the following principles for *giving* feedback.

- Distinguish between communicating an observation and judging it. These two messages should be communicated separately.

- Focus on sending "I-messages": "I perceive you as being too direct in your language and that makes me angry."

- One should directly communicate the intention or the wish to the feedback recipient:

  1. More – Keep going.
  2. Start – Add something to your behaviour (additional behaviour needed, more of the same, or less of the same).
  3. Stop – Avoid this behaviour.

In a global context, however, this Western feedback style may not be compatible with differing cultural preferences.

- In many cultures, especially in those where conflict is avoided, people are unlikely to separate content from relationship. Critical messages tend to have a negative impact on the relationship.

- In many cultures, especially in those with high context communication, direct language is not used to transmit messages. Instead, indirect language or omission is used to convey critical messages. Without taking context into account, decoding a message can therefore be very difficult.

Hence professional feedback in cross-cultural environments needs to follow different principles. We have identified two principal strategies to provide feedback with a positive impact. The first strategy can be called a no-regret measure. Here, the feedback process is optimized through applying Marshall B. Rosenberg's

No-regret feedback: A process model

principles of non-violent communication[*]. In light of the existing literature in this realm, suffice it here to offer a process model for applying this method when giving feedback.

1. State the observations that are leading you to feel the need to say something.

2. State the feeling that the observation is triggering in you. Or, guess what the other person is feeling, and ask.

3. State the need that is the cause of that feeling. Or, guess the need that caused the feeling in the other person, and ask.

4. Make a concrete request for action to meet the need just identified.

Creating a transcultural feedback culture

The other principle is based on the creation of a transcultural feedback culture built on the concept of exploiting diversity. This is about identifying the different feedback preferences of those involved in the feedback process (through voicing) and optimizing the process with this knowledge.

For both strategies, the starting point for improving a feedback culture can be either by

• sharing the individually perceived current state of an existing feedback practice; or

• sharing the individually desired optimal state of a feedback culture.

There are three ways to create a shared feedback culture[†].

---

[*] Rosenberg (2003).

[†] See Hildebrandt et al. (2013), chapter 1, for the distinction between monocultural, intercultural and transcultural.

The universal or monocultural approach

When applying a monocultural approach, people adapt to the preferences of the feedback giver or to the norms that are set by the organization or the dominant culture. This can be a "universally" valid set of behaviours ("Start by sharing your observation") or norms developed by a certain professional group.

The intercultural approach

Here, giving feedback adheres to the preferences of the person who receives the feedback.

The transcultural approach

The feedback partners or a whole group agree on mutually shared and attractive feedback practices leading to Resonant Feedback as one element of creating a shared collaboration space.

In the following, we will show how to create a transcultural approach to feedback.

Background: The Four Crystal Model

In 2011, Stefan Meister and Marcus Hildebrandt started researching international feedback practices (see Part IV: "Feedback in international contexts: results from our research", p. 289, for a summary of the results). Their research doesn't refer to institutional feedback as in an employee survey or an annual performance appraisal. "Feedback," as intended by them, refers to work-related, informal or formal responses that colleagues might spontaneously give each other, or as leaders might give to their colleagues or employees in a work context.

The Four Crystal Model

Research that led to the development of the Four Crystal Model included 1,000 data sets, 15 national cultures and two phases. The Four Crystal Model visualizes the central operational aspects associated with feedback practice. Resulting from more than two years of research into feedback practices among different cultures worldwide, the Four Crystal Model characterizes the main aspects of feedback practice and is backed by statistically relevant data. The purpose of the model – and the corresponding Feedback Profiler® questionnaire – is to help you and your work partners (including superiors, colleagues, subordinates, etc.) better understand preferences in giving and receiving "feedback" in a professional context. They provide a starting point for dialogue that can create a feedback culture that has a positive impact on workplace behaviours and leads to higher performance on an individual, tandem, group – and potentially organizational – level.

We call the type of feedback associated with these high performance states of communication "Resonant Feedback" (see also the definition above).

The Four Crystal Model is represented in four categories: drivers, setting, process and focus. Together, they represent 12 dimensions.

The first crystal of the model deals with the drivers of feedback.

Figure 2.20: Feedback drivers

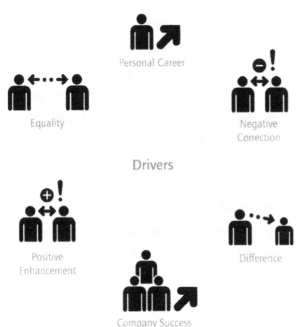

In other words, it analyses the circumstances that most likely motivate an individual to give (or receive) feedback: the purpose of feedback. More particularly, this first dimension examines what triggers the giving of feedback, especially if it is more performance-related or if it targets the personal development of the receiver. It also considers how the "level-difference" between feedback partners (e.g. hierarchy) or personal closeness influence the value of feedback for the person receiving it.

The second crystal examines the setting within which feedback is given and received.

Feedback setting

Figure 2.21: Feedback setting

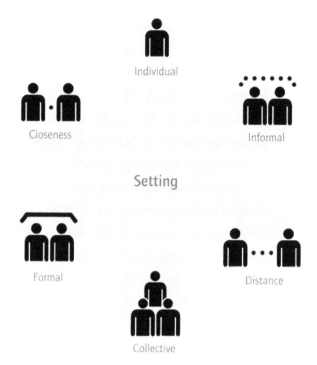

The questions asked in this category include where/in which context feedback is given and received, and who is present during the feedback. The physical environment, or actual space where communication is made, can be an office, conference room, restaurant or café, etc. The formality or informality of a given physical space is based on your own interpretation.

Setting also deals with the question of whether feedback is given in a more collectivistic or more individualistic context. It examines the importance of the group during a feedback process.

Once the drivers and setting have been considered, the third crystal investigates the process of feedback. This category targets the manner in which feedback is given, or the how of feedback.

Figure 2.22: Feedback process

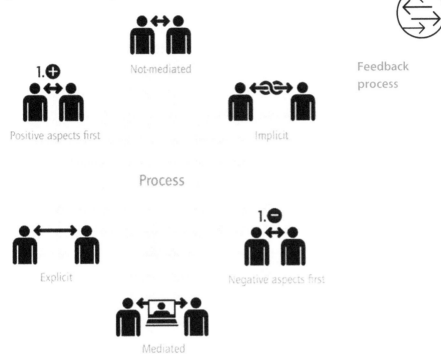

Feedback
process

Process

For example, is can be given in an implicit or explicit way. "Explicit" is intended to refer to a communication style that is relatively direct. Direct communicators tend to prefer to give and /or receive communication with stated intention. "Implicit" is intended to refer to a communication style that is relatively indirect. Indirect communicators tend to prefer to give and/or receive communication with an intention that is not verbalized.

Process also examines in which sequence feedback is given in a way that encourages positive aspects of behaviour or discourages negative aspects of behaviour. It also examines if feedback is delivered face-to-face, or mediated by a third person or by a certain technological medium (e.g. text-based, video/telephone conference, etc.).

Feedback focus

The final category takes care of the "what" concerning the feedback. It allows discussing preferences concerning the focus of the feedback. Would you like to get feedback on how you can improve your performance on a short time scale (e.g. focus on practical skills that can be easily learned) or are you more interested in feedback how to further develop in the long run (e.g. focus on behaviours or attitudes that are more difficult to change)? Are you more interested in feedback concerning the way you work or should there be primarily a focus on the results of your work?

Figure 2.23: Feedback focus

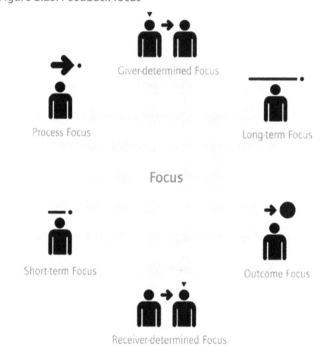

Sometimes it is better to let the feedback giver decide which focus he or she would prefer to take. Sometimes it is more effective if the feedback receiver decides the focus if he or she has decided on a certain area of personal development.

Collectively, the drivers, setting, process and focus crystals make up the Four Crystal Model.

Using the Feedback Profiler to achieve Resonant Feedback

The Feedback Profiler® is a diagnostic tool that enables the creation of a structured voicing process. The output is a visualization of the distribution of personal feedback preferences either on a 1:1 or group basis. The image below depicts the paper and pencil version of the Feedback Profiler®.

The Feedback Profiler®

Exhibit 2.5: Feedback Profiler

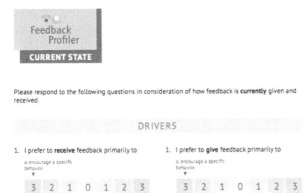

Typically, the output will be a spread of data visualizing the diversity of feedback preferences within a group.

The image below is an example from a workshop based on the paper and pencil version of the Feedback Profiler®.

Exhibit 2.6: Feedback Profiler applied

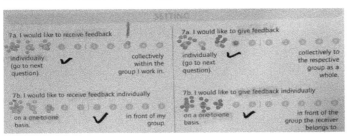

The Feedback Profiler® applied

It shows areas where the team can easily achieve consensus around shared feedback behaviours. But it also shows a great example of just one person having a different preference.

Classical facilitation would not really take this voice into account as it aims for majority approaches. In contrast to this we have developed other facilitation techniques in order to achieve results that are attractive for all stakeholders[*]. These techniques enable the person with the different preference to voice the need behind their preference. In our workshop example, the person had the impression that she didn't have a good standing within the group as she was rather new to the group. This decreased her motivation for receiving critical feedback. She preferred receiving positive feedback, including from her supervisor in front of the whole group.

This statement inspired the whole group to come up with what they called the default mode of feedback within their network:

- Encourage positive behaviour rather than pointing at negative behaviour.

- Critical feedback has to be constructive and conducive to personal development.

In most cases, however, the Feedback Profiler® produces outputs with less extreme cases and a larger spread of preferences as shown in the next image.

---

[*]   See Hildebrandt et al. (2013), chapter 7.

Exhibit 2.7: Drivers

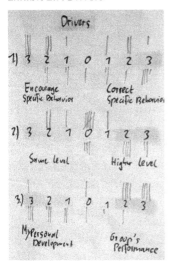

The Feedback Profiler® allows us to observe three generic categories of results that require different approaches.

1. All scores are on one side of the scale or at level 0. This basically means that the group can mutually agree on a rule, ideally in writing.

2. Nearly all scores are on one side of the scale or at level 0, but there are one or two deviations. This is the best opportunity for learning how to exploit diversity by applying the "hunting for the no" principle. There are one or two team members with different preferences. If the group went with the majority, they might risk losing valuable contributions from one or two of their members. If the person who has voted differently is willing to make this public within the group or in a 1:1 dialogue, the following questions will help to exploit the potential behind this vote.

   • First step: Appreciate that the person has the "guts" to address this. This is yet more potential for improving the voicing culture.
   • Second step: Find out about the context of this vote.

- Why did you vote this way? What is your interest/motivation behind it? What is preventing you from going along with what the others have suggested? Please give us some context around it in order to understand
- Third step: Pave the way towards a modified consensus.
    - What would help you to agree with the approach suggested by the others? Under what conditions could you imagine to go with the flow? What should be changed in order to enable you to agree?
- Fourth step: Take the new knowledge into account. There are three ways to do this:
    (1) Modify the rule so that everyone can agree. In our example, this could be: Feedback should be given individually and on a 1:1 basis. However, if you would like to praise someone who has done a great job, you can do so in front of the whole group.
    (2) If it's not possible to modify the approach so that everyone concerned can agree, say, "I am sorry but it looks like you have to live with this." In most cases this will work as the person has witnessed that you really tried to support his or her perspective or personal preferences.
    (3) Decide to make an exception of the rule for this person.

When addressing those who have indicated different preferences directly is not possible, the best way forward is forming small groups to work on this. Questions to be discussed may include:

- What might be the personal or cultural background behind this preference? What could be the motivation and interest behind it? What could hinder the person to go with the mainstream flow?

- What could help the person to agree to the approach of the others? What could be a modification that might support the person's agreeing with the majority?

Based on the results of their discussions, the groups will proceed to suggest modifications of the rules to which all can agree as well as measures that might help to live with the rule.

3. There are quite a number of cases with even distributions on both sides of the scale. Here it doesn't really make sense to try to agree on one approach. Instead it's useful to explore the perspectives behind the different preferences within the group to gain a better understanding. To that end, create a checklist to be addressed before feedback is given: Before giving feedback, please check with the person on your and/or their personal feedback preferences and tailor your feedback approach accordingly.

Summary

Building a voicing culture and a feedback culture is essential to the success of a diverse group in hyper-complex networks. Voicing will improve communication by establishing a practice of addressing anything that might potentially lead to miscommunication or conflict if left unattended. Regular Critical Incidents sessions are a great tool to help a group make voicing part of their daily professional life. As a specialized subset of voicing, a feedback culture demands tailored approaches to feedback in hyper-complex networks. Rather than employing Western style feedback, culturally diverse groups will greatly benefit from creating a transcultural feedback practice that caters to the different cultural preferences. The Feedback Profiler® is a potent tool to support groups in doing so.

Influencing the organization

Interview with Xavier Randretsa

Human Resources Director for IT

Figure 2.24: Xavier Randretsa's complexity image

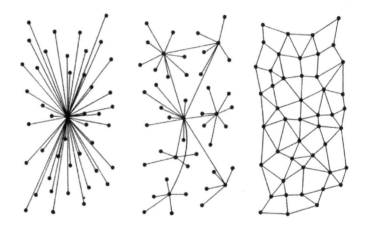

Profile
- ❖ Division HR Director
- ❖ French
- ❖ 49 years old
- ❖ Married, three children
- ❖ Responsible for 1,200 people in 23 countries and networking with 12 HR managers in USA, Mexico, Portugal, Tunisia, France, Germany, India, China, etc.

Xavier Randretsa is head of HR for IT at an international Automotive tier one supplier group that counts 20 B€ in sales revenue and 100,000 employees at 320 sites worldwide. Xavier has held numerous functions in HR at large industrial groups, growing step by step from specialist roles (training, recruitment, career development, industrial relations) to generalist HR roles, advancing from manager to business partner to director. Xavier is pragmatic, results oriented and focused on international organizations, supporting middle managers and teams at site level. "My task is not only to control that policies are implemented, but mainly to support and coach the middle managers, the key change agents, to generate results impacting collective performance."

The complexity wherein Xavier operates

Xavier emphasizes that organizations are becoming increasingly global and complex. "Even dealing with a matrix organization is not easy when the functional manager is abroad." His organizational environment is characterized by two main dimensions of complexity. On the one hand, the company holds competence centres mainly in high-cost countries like France, Germany and the USA). These hubs are dedicated to globally leading an activity or domain or technology. They own projects, budgets, processes and standards. On the other hand, Shared Services Centres are spread across low-cost countries. They are tasked with supporting local growth and application of the policies set out by the Competence Centres, focusing either on a country or a region. When local solutions do not suffice, they receive support from the global Competence Centres.

"The challenge for the Competence Centres is developing the autonomy of our local teams at the in Mexican, Portuguese, Tunisian, Czech or Chinese Shared Services Centres at a distance. Natural constraints such as different time zones, cultural and behavioural differences and even a bad 'Globish' language are used to justify incomplete delivery and not respecting deadlines."

How much of your company is family, machine or network? How much of your job is family, machine or network?

Table 2.3: Xavier Randretsa's complexity mix

	The whole group	IT organization
Network	10%	10%
Machine	80%	60%
Family	10%	30%

"Our company, being part of the automotive industry, is a typical matrix organization and entirely process oriented and focused on building excellence in operations on worldwide standards. Small and autonomous teams are developed at plant level where workers are trained in instructions, core procedures and formal security mandatory rules before being certified internally on a regular basis."

The IT organization of the company is a mix of standardized matrix processes and family culture. This makes sense given that historically, IT requires that specialists talk to specialists. "More importantly, our experts at the Competence Centres welcome new employees during the induction and training period. Through business trips and regular workshops people are encouraged to develop a sense of belonging to the IT family. However, while the Digital Enterprise and the Company Social Network are opening new spaces of collaboration, we are slow to develop networks across IT communities and the whole organization."

Xavier's strategies to reduce and navigate this complexity: What has worked and what hasn't worked so well, and why?

Xavier explains how, based on his previous experience as head of learning at the Corporate University, he discovered that all team managers who were exposed for the first time to people management were facing the same problems and questions across all countries. How to delegate? How to refocus a more experienced colleague? How to animate and motivate the team? How to detect changes in individual behaviour and whether they are due to work-related or personal issues? How to get feedback? How to dedicate time to support and coach team members?

"So, in addition to the constraints due to distance, we had to find a simple way to introduce a new common space of belonging for isolated or split team members. This included building proximity through trust, defining rules for communication within the team, providing knowledge to better use existing technologies and rebuilding the same team management practice as is used by collocated teams. For this to happen, training middle and top managers in the appropriate methodology and tools was in order."

Distant Management training

Coinciding with the launch of a new company culture in 2014, and promoting the development of autonomy and accountability, Xavier was introduced to Line Jehle at perform-globally.com. This meeting came after a first and unsuccessful attempt at designing a Distant Management training. "We had wanted to integrate all the elements that we had identified into a training cocktail for successful distant management. These included some input on team management, some intercultural tips, some highlights of using media and some serious games and case studies.

Unfortunately, the mix had no taste and nothing changed as participants went back to work.

Line Jehle immediately recognized the excess of complexity of the training design. She introduced a mere two sentences that made 'Tilt!' in our heads:

- Create a new space of belonging, where people feel close and together and pleasure when being connected.

- Use technology to simulate reality.

Within ten minutes, my boss, VP CIO of our group, and I were convinced to launch a training with a pilot session for senior management.

The most visible improvements, starting at senior management level, have included:

- Different conduction of the bi-monthly meetings. Previously, half of the team were meeting in the same room in France while the other half were connecting individually and separately from different countries. We also introduced new meeting rules, chiefly by introducing the concept of rotating e-facilitation. A different team member would take on the role of moderator in each meeting, ensuring that all participants listen and participate. The result was a shared feeling of greater equality among participants as they were all using the same technological setup (conference call with shared screen) and taking more collective decisions instead of succeeding individual speeches.

- An improved voicing of tensions to curb emotions and avoid jumping to solutions too quickly. With exemplarity being one of our six corporate values, we understood that if the approach worked at top management level, it was likely to be successful at every management level and to solicit greater alignment of hierarchical and functional managers, speaking one voice in front of the employee."

Xavier's reactions to the central parameters of leading in the face of hyper-complexity

- <u>Shaping and influencing organizational communities</u> – Yes. Encouraging company-wide social networking and rewarding community leaders who promote innovation as an added value for the business.

- <u>Creating virtual closeness and global collaboration spaces</u> – Yes. This is one of the two key points, even if "virtual" may have a negative connotation. I would prefer "creating proximity and closeness with a new collaboration space".

- <u>Framework setting and mastering technology</u> – Yes. Media competence must be developed. Managers need to learn when to use synchronous or asynchronous media depending on the purpose of communication (brainstorming, top-down information sharing, giving and receiving feedback, etc.).

- <u>Dealing with complexity</u> – Yes. We need to do everything to simplify how we deal with a complex organization when we cannot simplify the organization itself.

- <u>Personal branding</u> – Yes. All team members need to be visible to each other by creating an online identity.

- <u>Contextual leadership</u> – Intercultural competence can greatly facilitate leadership. For example, to be able to solicit expected behaviours from a Chinese or an American the leader would need to adapt his communication style. But this alone is not enough. They also need to be empathetic and know how to coach and be visible and available when required across different time zones.

- <u>Creating a culture of voicing</u> – Yes. This is the other key point.

- <u>Measuring success</u> – Yes. Reward, congratulate and celebrate even the small successes with the entire team.

Influencing the organization

"Those who have only a hammer as a tool perceive any problem as a nail."

The mental model we have of an organization and its dynamics significantly dictates our approach to working with the organization. Paul Watzlawick once said, "Those who have only a hammer as a tool perceive any problem as a nail."*

Usually, at the beginning of an Organization Development process, we ask our clients to draw a picture of the organization or their organizational context as they perceive it. The pictures are always very different. We then either ask participants what they associate with the pictures before everyone explains their mental models. Or we, the consultants, share our regular observation that local teams are represented by solid squares which are connected with other round or square solid containers housing other colleagues.

This compartmentalizing mental model makes setting up global networks and sharing knowledge globally rather difficult.

Similarly, when we ask participants to draw a picture of a (their) social network the following drawing is rather typical.

---

* „Wer als Werkzeug nur einen Hammer hat, sieht in jedem Problem einen Nagel."

Figure 2.24: Mental models of networks

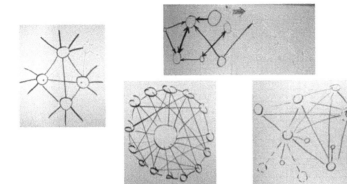

These pictures fail to capture the essential features formed by the inner dynamics of social and all other organically growing networks that lead to both hubs and weak links (see Part IV: "The concepts of groups, networks and communities, p. 269, and "Principles of communication and their connection to network and community dynamics", p. 287)*.

This is why at the beginning of any attempt to shape or at least influence an organization or a unit thereof, one has to challenge one's own and all others' implicit assumptions and mental models that are at work.

Understanding the mental models at work in an organization

What about you? We invite you to draw a picture of your organization or your organizational context and ask outsiders what they see or associate with your picture and what emotions your picture invokes. You may receive responses along the lines of the following. "I have the impression that this big red square on top is heavily weighing on the little circles underneath, creating a lot of pressure. I wonder how these affiliates feel towards headquarters. By the way, I miss the word/element *customer* in your picture. Why is that?"

---

*   Albert et al. (2000).

Later in this chapter, we will offer you a more structured approach for challenging and possibly reshaping your mental model or that of your co-workers.

The macroscopic perspective on leading network organizations

In the previous chapters, we have taken a rather microscopic look at leading networks and engaging with members' local contexts. In this chapter, we will switch to a macroscopic perspective on dealing with larger chunks of an organization. This chapter is therefore dedicated to those leaders who steer and drive the organization on a higher level and who are in charge of multiple and diverse teams and several business networks.

Xavier Randretsa is a good example of a leader who understands the importance of using technology to simulate reality. He is a role model in using new media and understands that as a leader leading by example, he can push for increased media competence in his organization. He encourages company-wide social networking. For him, influencing is intimately connected to innovation, and he believes in rewarding community leaders who promote innovation as an added value for the business.

Self-similarity and tipping points

That said, the principle of self-similarity[*] of complex as well as hyper-complex systems means that the patterns that appear on a microscopic scale also exist on the macroscopic level. In addition, new features, especially collective phenomena that are absent on the micro level, do emerge on the macro level. An example of this is the

---

[*] A self-similar system shows the same structures and shapes on all hierarchical levels, for example empowerment on individual, team and organizational levels. Alternatively, the whole has the same shape as one or more of the parts, such as a central structure in a team, a local and a global organization.

phenomenon of collective resonance leading to tipping points and transitional processes in societies[*].

Examples of macro-societal patterns unfolding globally as we write this include, for example, Russia that is drifting away from the "West". Another example may be seen in the dramatically increasing mass migration to the European Union and its impact on the concept of pluralistic societies and local cultures.

While these phenomena are ancient elements of human evolution, we now possess the analytical knowledge to understand the underlying dynamics, at least in principle. Yet, the world remains a mysterious place and we can't understand it fully and maybe never will.

Nonetheless we would like to share with you in the following some practical ideas and experiences of influencing and shaping global network organizations on a macro level with the purpose of increasing the organization's ability to innovate.

Defining influencing an organization

Human network systems that evolve mainly in a self-organized manner are strongly sensitive

- to the framework in which the system is embedded (the "boundary conditions"); and

- to positive resonance created by attractive options, opportunities, people (see chapter "Leadership branding", p. 65) or more abstract elements within the system.

Taking this into account, developing a successful community website starts with creating a home page that polarizes

---

[*] Gladwell (2001).

Creating
network hubs:
groups of people
who gather
around topics

people. They either love the colours, the fonts, the general layout and the structure and navigation of the site or they are repelled by it*. The challenge is, of course, to ensure the target group of the website finds it attractive. If this succeeds, the "the-winner-takes-it-all" dynamics of exponential growth within social networks is initiated (see also the "bubble principle" in the interview with Arnulf Keese, p. 96). The more members you start out with, the more you attract new ones. This leads to a runaway effect with the result that all members of a group use only a small number of websites.

The Internet is the best example for this phenomenon. There are the giants like Google, Facebook, Alibaba, YouTube, WordPress or Flickr and the billions of other websites that are barely noticed, let alone used. The former are hubs, the main entry points to the Internet that are extremely powerful in influencing and connecting people. Hubs are nodes or intersections that bundle attractiveness and whose purpose draws large majorities of people. In global network organizations, hubs take over global core functions such as human resources or legal affairs. Hubs are groups of people that gather around topics.

Social network hubs also explain the "Small World Phenomenon", also known as the Theory of Six Degrees of Separation, which holds that all inhabitants of this planet are connected to each other through a chain of six people on average.

Increasing
transparency
through
changing the
framework

When networks grow too large, it becomes very difficult if not impossible to steer them. Hence a well-structured framework is necessary to manage and organize interactions. Changing such a framework may lead to new patterns in the system.

Andrew Parker[†] has explained the explosion of diversity

---

* Kim (2006).
† Parker (2003).

in the oceans about 550 million years ago, during the Cambrian era, with the fact that the transparency of the oceans was increasing. The animals were developing new senses that could better process light, a development that eventually led to the existence of the eye. This also dramatically changed the relationship between predators and their prey. Animals suddenly tried to protect themselves either from being seen (camouflage) or by developing a biological shield that is hard to break and bite through.

We may experience similarly abrupt changes and new patterns on the Internet when data transparency continues to increase[*].

By definition, self-organizing systems change their framework in a way that is either favourable or disastrous for the system in the long run. In the early days of life on earth, anaerobic bacteria were consuming carbon dioxide and produced oxygen as a waste product. They ended up in a world dominated by oxygen, limiting their existence to very restricted places. With industrialization, however, we may be going back to the times of these bacteria as we continue to produce carbon dioxide by burning oxygen in our engines and power plants.

We have now identified the following main aspects of influencing an organization on the macro level.

The five main aspects of influencing organizations

1. Examining mental models of the organizational context

Challenge and possibly reshape your mental model of your context and the organization by moving away from thinking in terms of processes, departments, functions and tasks and focusing instead on individuals and contents.

2. Creating an attractive initiative

---

[*] Dennett, Roy (2015).

Create an attractive initiative that is visible throughout the organization and has an impact on the system. Be attractive and visible.

3. Setting the framework

Shape the framework so that it promotes certain behavioural patterns and useful weak signals.

4. Using the intrinsic dynamics of the system

Use the intrinsic dynamics of the system and of existing hubs to create, spread and reinforce desired patterns.

5. Honing contextual intelligence

Hone your contextual intelligence to adjust your moves (see chapter "Contextual leadership", p. 93).

Let's now turn to examining in detail how to implement these aspects.

How to influence organizations

In the following, we will elaborate the first four of the five aspects introduced above and illustrate each with a case vignette from our work with organizations and leaders. Contextual intelligence is discussed in the chapter "Contextual leadership" (p. 93).

The interviews presented in Part III shed further light on how some managers influence their organizations.

1. Examining mental models of the organizational context

To draw out the conceptions managers have of their hyper-complex work environments, we ask them to map their global task network. Here are some example results.

Exhibits 2.8–2.10: Mapping global task networks 1

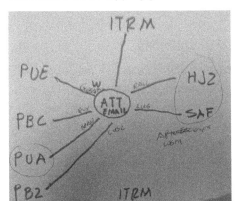

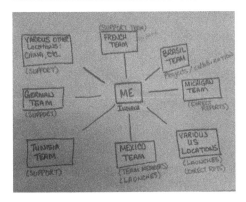

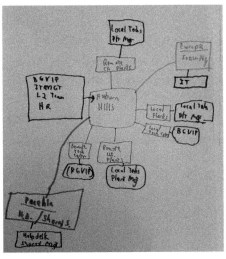

Exercise 1

Map your global task network.

Mapping your
global task
network

These drawings capture the disorientation or loss of focus that most managers experience when addressing their hyper-complex work environments. Memorizing one's own role and relation to each section of any of these charts is alone a daunting task.

From the sketches, we can derive that these managers have their hands full. Their drawings made clear our purpose for writing this book. Take a look at the pictures. What do you notice? These charts are chaotic, dispropor-tionate, and disconnected – all hindrances to successfully reducing a context's complexity to the core that you can really manage und use to influence your context.

Networks are by nature unstructured due to their unlimited variables. It then stands to reason that these hand-drawn graphs struggle to find structure, too. Many managers find this lack of structure somewhat frustrating. Although networks cannot be sorted into traditional charts used by machine systems, they, too, can become easier to handle if the manager learns to move away from thinking in departments, functions, locations and tasks and learns to think in forms of elements and structures that are more appropriate in networks: individuals, hubs and weak links (see Part IV: "The concepts of groups, networks and communities, p. 269, for further informa-tion on this).

In most cases, managers who are experts at running highly structured environments, tend to map their work environment with connections to departments that are to fulfil their specific demands. But as we already pointed out in several parts of the book we have to shift from clas-sical task orientation to orientation towards individuals within their context and sense making. The local office far away from the site of the manager has a stack of local work to get done, and since they feel little connection to you or your initiative/objectives, they are going to cover their own backs before they take time out to see to your needs. This is why it is crucial for a manager to focus on making connections with people rather than jobs that need to be done.

If you seek out specific people within the offices of importance and build their interest in your work, then it is more likely that they will personally see that the task get completed by someone under their jurisdiction. These few, strong relationships are how one creates closeness in a global network*.

Without a shared space between those involved in the project, the managers become the middle men, placing all the stress of communication and problem-solving on themselves and leaving their partners feeling disconnected from the project and its goals (see also Part IV: "Principles of communication and their connection to network and community dynamics", p. 287, for some basic axioms of network communication).

Thus as a manager, one should aim to build a small core (possibly in the form of a team) of key players within the given work context, who can advocate for the network's needs to fulfil the purpose within their own realm of business relations. In forming such a global core (-team), we can hope to develop closeness with the other members in a way that will allow the leadership initiative to maintain focus, strive for efficiency and promote growth.

---

*   Hildebrandt et al. (2013), chapter 1.

Exhibits 2.11–2.13: Mapping global task networks 2

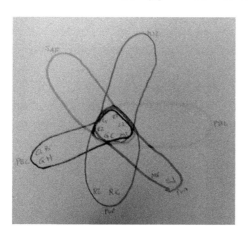

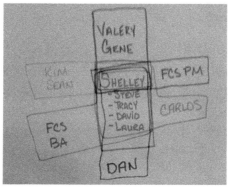

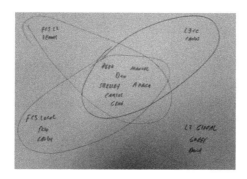

Exercise 2

Compare this set of charts to the original sketches. Which set would you rather have as your work reality? Now it is your turn, go and change your original chart. While doing so, focus on picking a core structure (possibly a team or a community) which makes your global project feel local.

2. Creating an attractive initiative

If the purpose or the objectives of an initiative are not absolutely clear to all stakeholders beyond cultural differences, it is difficult to get a real response to it. The first step is therefore to work on this issue.

Here is a case vignette from an energy provider.

Critical Knowledge Management at an Energy Provider

A leader was tasked with improving the intensity and quality of knowledge management within a larger global unit of engineers who are in charge of running the complex turbines and other technical settings of power plants on a multinational scale.

Case vignette: Knowledge management

In our role as consultants we suggested that "knowledge management" is merely a catchy phrase just like "the learning organization". Such fashionable terminology has no intrinsic value if there is no clear purpose or business pain providing a context in which one can apply these methods. Moreover, these phrases have no clear and transcultural meaning on the behavioural level.

We advised the leadership team to identify critical situations that cause business pain and in which knowledge management is critical to finding solutions. One of these issues was turbine failure.

We proceeded to identify clear behavioural manage-ment expectations for instances of turbine failure. First, approaches to dealing with turbine failure need to lead to an improved knowledge transfer between sites. Second, they have to be attractive for the community members.

The key to making these management expectations attrac-tive for community members was to understand that

- there is a global engineering ethos that is based on certain values engineers share, and

- that engineers are usually very proud of their local solutions.

We agreed that any initiative that fails to respect these core elements might not lead to a sustained process of collaboration and knowledge sharing.

Leadership came up with the following set of expected behaviours, which they presented to the community and got its buy-in.

1. In case of turbine failure, the local team will analyze the issue and come up with a solution or a set of measures to the best of their knowledge. This step acknowledges local wisdom and pride and values and demonstrates trust in the competences of the local team.

2. The local team presents its results to at least one other power plant outside of the organizational unit for feedback. This step supports knowledge exchange and helps establish a practice of constructive feed-back that can extend to other areas of cooperation. It also fuels the local team's drive to create the best possible solution and motivates the other team to add value by finding possible technical pitfalls.

3. Management will only accept and implement those solutions that were signed off by both teams.

This is an example of a set of so-called "non-negotiable behaviours" that are clear in any cultural context[*].

Our advice is to create such a set of attractive behaviours at the beginning of any leadership initiative, or to probe the system to identify the desired behaviours while moving along. To initiate a positive spiral dynamics, the desired behaviours need to be reinforced by making them visible to others and appreciating them in a transparent way within the community.

3. Setting the framework

In our book "Closeness at a Distance", we introduced the concept of a shared cooperation space that is attractive for the team or network members and reduces the complexity of members' interactions[†]. We called this the "purple space" to emphasize that it results from blending the different cultural (national and organizational) colours that exist within a group. We also introduced methods and techniques that support facilitation processes in these "purple spaces"[†].

Global cooperation spaces

While our focus there was on the micro level and on cultural issues, we will now have a closer look at the organizational level and the concept of purpose-driven purple spaces.

One central leadership task is to devote time and energy to developing a framework that fosters self-organization and shared leadership. As early as possible, leaders need to decide which elements of this framework should be fixed by executive decision and which ones can be co-created in a participative process together with the network.

---

[*] Herrero (2008).

[†] Hildebrandt et al. (2013), chapter 1.

[‡] For example, the "hunting for the no" technique or the principle of Deep Democracy, see p. 146.

The following case study demonstrates how this can be done.

In the example, management was asked to create a purple space to promote and improve communication and cross-fertilization processes between different experts within a unit in order to increase synergies in handling complex projects and processes. Most of the unit members had previously worked in expert teams, where silo thinking and little interaction characterized the interaction between teams. See also Part IV: "Principles of communication and their connection to network and community dynamics", p. 287, for some basic axioms of network communication.

Case study team/network: Roles and responsibilities in teams versus purpose and identity in networks and communities

A new organizational unit with about 42 experts was formed. The experts had previously either worked in teams or alone.

Within the new unit, the five "old" teams were used as crystallization points around which other formerly "team free" members could coalesce. All members were allocated to one of these five teams which now housed a richer variety of topics.

Each of these five teams has a team leader. Two of the team leaders (one man and one woman) represent the unit which is headed by one person, a woman.

Our job was to coach the head of the unit and to support her in developing the unit on an organizational level.

While there were tasks on which only one team would work (coming from outside stakeholders and interfaces), in the future there were going to be projects or processes on which the entire unit would work. The challenge was to create a structure and processes that allow for the synergetic coexistence of the team on the one hand, and an overall network/community structure that is able to handle joint projects and processes for the outside market as well as provide dedicated solutions to interfaces within the organization on a team level on the other hand.

Here is how we approached this challenge.

After a long discussion with the group of team leaders and the unit head we all agreed that the first step would be to create a sense of belonging for every person in the unit. This step would also help to clarify roles and responsibilities within the team.

In addition, we decided to pilot a joint project on which the entire unit would work to ensure that the teams would not lose their outside focus and their functional embedding in the larger organizational unit. The group voted for a project based on a choice of projects given by the unit leader. The purpose of this project was to help every individual to identify with the network/community unit and define the purpose for collaborating outside of their team context.

During some of the first interventions we worked with the whole group on a team level. Every team was asked to create its own team spirit. Who are we? What competences and projects do we have currently in our team? Where do we find synergies and what makes us unique within the unit? What are our services/offers to the unit? Moreover, every team was asked to agree on its heartbeat, meaning the frequency of synchronous meetings, and a decision-making structure.

After this process all teams presented their results.

In a next step, the head of the unit introduced the project the group as a whole had chosen. As an important detail, the whole group, sitting as the five respective teams around five tables, was asked to give feedback on the project idea and to voice unfiltered feelings, concerns and ideas around the project. Some people voiced concerns about the workload, some said that they really liked the project idea, yet others suggested to rephrase the core topic of the process as the title had a slightly negative connotation in their opinion.

As a result of the discussion the title was changed to a more attractive one with which all could identify. Also, it was stated that the joint project would not add to the teams' existing workloads. To that end, the teams were asked to creatively "recycle" their existing services and products for internal and external customers.

Next, the teams were asked to work on the joint project and, specifically, on the following questions. What is our vision within this project (as a team)? What makes us unique? Which products and services can our team offer to the joint project? Where do we see interfaces to the other teams? What do we need from the other teams in order to be able to deliver?

The results of this step were presented as a gallery.

In a final round, we identified shared statements based on the answers to the question, "What is our vision within this project?", and created a shared identity. We also created a headline from the teams' respective contributions to the joint project.

During the feedback session, people shared their relief about finding ways to balance workloads. They were looking forward to learning about the different perspectives on the joint project.

In terms of communication, they agreed on a regular heartbeat of biweekly synchronous meetings to address the joint project needs. Each team would decide autonomously who was to represent it in that meeting, either the team leader or one or several experts. Furthermore, there would be a monthly meeting between the team leaders and the unit head.

The teams themselves agreed on weekly or biweekly internal meetings.

4. <u>Using the intrinsic dynamics of the system</u>

One inherent feature of all open social systems is that they evolve, always developing towards the optimum within the given framework. This is part of the evolutionary process. The hidden rules that an organization is based on are direct indicators for this.

The question is therefore not how to create a dynamic but rather, in which direction the system is evolving and whether the framework allows for the emergence of stable patterns or for the decay of undesired patterns.

Working with the internal dynamics allows for an efficient and sustained impact on the organization, while ignoring them is one of the root causes for the failure of change management.

So far, little practical knowledge about this exists. However, we would like to share with you a relevant experience one of us has acquired in this field together with another partner.

OPR: A new approach to organizational development

Jobst Scheuermann and Marcus Hildebrandt have developed a new approach to organizational development in general with an application to change management.

Their idea is to make use of the inner dynamics and the framework in which a system is embedded. They call their new approach Optimization – Polarity – Resonance (OPR)[*]. It takes into account the interplay between

- the objectives one wants to achieve,

- the framework in which the development is embedded, and

- the inner dynamics of the system.

OPR seeks to expand those approaches to change management that don't take the dynamic coupling of these three elements fully into account[†].

Here is how OPR works.

OPR is intended for leadership initiatives that are meant to stir an organization up and are purpose driven ("optimization"). As explained earlier, such stirring requires probing within the context and then fine-tuning and adjusting while acting.

One knows that one's initiative makes a difference if it causes visible polarity. Some people will show a "towards" behaviour, others will display an "away" mode (see chapter "Contextual leadership", p. 112). Where there is light there is always shadow. This also implies that an initiative needs reshaping if it doesn't show the desired

---

[*]   Scheuermann, Hildebrandt (2015).
[†]   See, for example, Herrera (2008).

reaction, or is cancelled before a lot of time and money is wasted. This is where OPR differs from other approaches that suggest applying more force and power to break the system's resistance.

Figure 2.25: Polarities within the organization

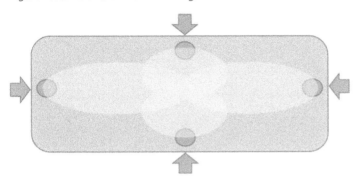

This (multi-) polarity is a natural reaction of any system to being stirred up. It causes the tension that is needed to create a dynamic and the corresponding dynamic attractors that point in the desired direction.

If the framework is the right one and the initiative is attractive for the different stakeholders and key people, the system will meet with a resonance that overcomes the polarities.

Figure 2.26: A leadership initiative creates resonance on all levels of the organization

Pictured below is a more detailed flow chart on how to apply OPR.

Figure 2.27: OPR

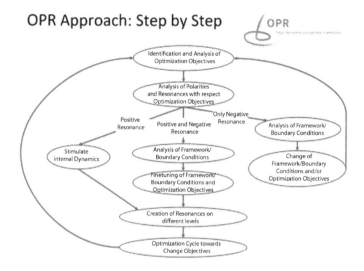

Summary

When setting out to influence an organization on the macro level, five main aspects need to be taken into account: examining the existing mental models of the organizational context; creating attractive leadership initiatives; setting a framework that promotes relevant behavioural patterns; using the system's intrinsic dynamics; and honing one's contextual intelligence.

Part III: Personal mixes and recipes

Introduction

While all of us are probing and fine-tuning our approaches in ever-increasing hyper-complexity, it may offer a bit of comfort that we are not alone in this. In fact, anybody leading in the face of these challenges is a pioneer of sorts and from these insights all of us can be inspired.

It was in this spirit of learning that we interviewed the ten global leaders from a wide range of organizational, professional and cultural backgrounds whose voices you find collected in this book.

We kicked off each chapter in Part II ("Dealing with your complexity mix") with an essay that is essentially an executive summary of an interview with one of these leaders that directly touched upon a theme or topic particularly relevant to the respective chapter.

The interviews integrated in the following section are intentionally presented in a different format. Here we kept almost the complete interview in its original flow in order to give you more contextual cues on how

- the interview partners communicated their statements;

- they were partly probing for their answers;

- they sometimes also shared personal weaknesses or failures;

- their leadership branding might be felt.

From this you will gain a more holistic view of the person behind the text. This might help you to experience these leaders in more differentiated ways and to learn from and with them more easily. There are, of course, no right or wrong answers.

We are all very thankful to all interview partners who gave us very personal insights into their way of perceiving their complexities, their professional contexts, and their leadership approaches.

Interview with Stephen Karnik: Trust never sleeps

Figure 3.1: Stephen Karnik's complexity image

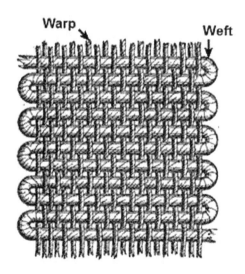

Stephen explains why he chose this image: "The image of woven cloth comes to mind when thinking about complexity in my work. The blending and interweaving of threads to form a strong, integrated and cohesive fabric, which supports organization and its mission. The "warp" being the individual tasks/ responsibilities/ operations/ logistics/ mechanics with the "woof" or in this image the "weft" being the human dimensions/ qualities/ considerations/ real people/ guiding and foundational principles. Without the woof, the warp has no cohesion, strength or form. It becomes a collection of isolated tasks lacking integration/ coordination/ purpose/ strength."

Name: Stephen Karnik

Education: Master's degree in non-profit administration

Nationality: US-American

Employment history:

- He has been with the Baha'i International Community now for just under 20 years

- He was originally working out of Israel and then transferred to New York a number of years ago

- His earliest work was in community organization and working with primarily poverty agencies in the United States

Current Position:

- Chief administrative officer for the Baha'i International Community's operations, mostly in terms of administration and programme design, planning and development

Interviewer: It is wonderful that you are taking this time to share your experiences of how to deal with what we would tend to call hyper-complexity. In terms of introduction, what do you think might be interesting for our readers to know about you?

Stephen: Right now professionally I am the chief administrative officer for the Baha'i International Community's operations. They consist of five offices serving different entities. Working with the United Nations, we have our main office in New York. We have another office in Geneva and three regional offices. One is in Brussels which follows issues not only in Europe but specifically also interacts with the various European Union entities. In Addis Ababa, we have another regional office, that one follows the African Union, as well as other issues in Africa. And our most recent office is in Jakarta, Indonesia, which follows South East Asian activities.

Interviewer: Maybe for those readers who don't know, could you please explain what the Baha'i Faith is?

Stephen: The Baha'i International Community is the operational entity that represents the members and entities of the Baha'i Faith in an international context, mostly in a diplomatic context, and also just in terms of the external affairs and external representations of the Baha'i community globally. So there are 5.5 – 6 million Baha'is, spread out quite diversely throughout the world. We do not make a separation between religious communities or faiths. We just view them as all stages in a continuing process, of which the Baha'i Faith is not the end. The most recent teachings of the Baha'i Faith, originating in the mid-19th century, are geared towards the establishment of a global society.

Interviewer: Great. You have already given a key term, which is global.

Stephen: And global for us is essential. And that is really one of the pivots around which our religious teachings focus. We have an expression, which is very simple but with incredible depth to it: 'mankind is one'.

Interviewer: Stephen, looking at the complexity that you are moving through in terms of acting globally, can you share what exactly does this mean for your role as a leader? Do you directly lead people? And how many are they? Where are they? How do you communicate with them and how do you lead them? Is there something like in business with dotted and solid lines?

Stephen: What we are looking at is a network of the five primary offices. All of the administrative, financial and technological aspects of them are my domains as well as the human resource aspect. We are making sure that all of those elements are working in an integrated and coordinated way to move the entire organization forward as seamlessly as possible. Then, in addition to that, we are covering really extensive topical portfolios. So we are looking at gender issues, a range of human rights issues, climate issues, poverty eradication, inequality, sustainable development, social development. That far exceeds our staffing resources, in terms of the representatives and our research staff – we have a small research capability as well. We utilize a network of individuals in different parts of the world with various expertise to assist with our following of the various portfolios, and that introduces another layer of complexity because these are primarily volunteers. So you are kind of juggling their availability and trying to maintain them as engaged and active supporters of the work that you are doing. We also have internally a network of interns that we utilize. They are drawn from different parts of the world. Currently in our office at this very moment, we have two individuals from India, one from Mozambique and one from Australia.

Interviewer: So all in all, what would you say, how many people are reporting directly to you and how many are, like the volunteers, connected with dotted lines that you may need to influence differently?

Stephen: Here in New York, we would have 14. In our Geneva office we would have four. Our regional offices are fairly small and new. In Brussels there is one. In Addis Ababa there are currently two and one in Jakarta, about to become two. Our networks are intern-based, between New York and Geneva at any point in time, I would say we have about six. Our broader networks of external resources vary. These volunteers would probably be in the vicinity of about 20 in different parts of the world. Even the US operations are actually in three locations.

Interviewer: If you look at the three organizational paradigms Family, Machine, Network, can you recognize one or two or even all three in your organization?

Stephen: I think the first and the third primarily. The machine is the least but an element, nonetheless. And just looking at them, I think to me the most interesting is the first, the family. Each of these external offices has a different focus, the organization still needs to speak as a single entity because this is a representation of a global community and, though we have different environments and different contexts, the voice needs to be the same. So one of the concerns is really, how do you maintain an environment where people are able to be on the same page while dealing with very different issues and have that sort of continuity, but still have the degree of flexibility that is required for them to operate in their various contexts? And so you are juggling a lot of various human issues. On the one hand, from my perspective, how do I keep individuals – if I take Brussels or Jakarta, for example, where these individuals are alone, how do I keep them from feeling isolated? How do I keep them engaged when so often, particularly in an environment like this, so much of what is happening is conceptual? What happens when the person is 5,000 miles away? And they are going to local meetings and they are coming back to their office and they have themselves. So you are looking at how you maintain that sense of connectedness. Part of what we use to a great degree is web conferencing. We do this in a number of ways and have certain regular web consultations and as long as people's schedules permit, they are active participants. That helps a great deal. On Wednesday mornings, for example, we found a time that gives us the best reach for the most people with different time zones. So we are able to coordinate our meeting times to enable the greatest number of people to participate. And we have what we call a coordination meeting, which gives people a chance to really exchange information. It is not about what they are doing – there are other formats for doing that – but about to bring issues to the table that they are trying to draw input from the broader group: Look, here is what I am facing right now. There is also a significant amount of bilateral communication, as people are working on specific issues. Frequently much of that is also web conferencing. We have found it is easier to sustain the engagement over an extended period of time when there is visual connection. If people have just a voice coming from an object on the table they are doing other things while they are following the conversation, to various degrees. And when you are having a two-hour audio meeting it is very difficult. All of the workstations are equipped in a way to handle web conferencing. That helps a great deal but it is not enough though. I tailor my schedule to accommodate the time zones. We do a lot in off-hours, just to make sure that people feel connected. I have a policy that whenever there is an issue anywhere, in any of our offices, they will all just call, no matter what time it is. But I spend a fair amount of time, very conscious time, in contact with all of the offices, not for any specific business issue or question. It is a matter of maintaining a human connection and being connected to the people apart from questions like: What do you need today? What is your problem? What is your issue? Part of this is also the tone you have, when you get that call, at the odd hour. My particular approach is, that it can never be annoyance. It is always like: Oh, good to hear from you. What can I do for you? How can I help?

Interviewer: So what I have learned is that you are using a wide range of methods to deal with the complexity you are facing. You are, for example, succeeding in creating virtual closeness. You are also doing excellent framework setting providing and promoting certain media. You are inviting to meetings at regular intervals, so people have a certain rhythm, what we would call heartbeat. How are you engaging the volunteers, giving them enough attractive reasons to be there when you need them?

Stephen: This is really the key. I have noticed in other environments I have been in, that this is where the ball is frequently dropped because the need to nurture and sustain your volunteer network is really critical. They will pass on an assignment, step back and wait for the assignment to come in and maybe after some time lose interest and drop off. This is a primary uniqueness that we have. You would find it in any group of volunteers that have a real commitment to an issue. Since we are a religious community, there is that unique relationship that we have to the majority of our volunteers who are also members of the Baha'i community. So from that perspective, there is something that we can draw upon in terms of building a connection. And then you need to sustain that connection. And part of this is human contact. We use the web conferencing as often as we can because the visuals really help. It gives them an opportunity to talk about their weekly work with others who are engaged in other aspects of a particular issue and process. There is kind of learning going on. After an event has ended, for example like the climate conference in Paris, you do not want to necessarily sever that connection. So how do I sustain them outside of that? And that is again where that personal contact comes in. But it is also helpful for them to see the value of their contribution. It is not an optional thing. It is not just a value-added. It is an essential aspect. It is about keeping them connected to the product.

Interviewer: Stephen, we've defined central elements we think really make up hyper-complexity. I invite you to say 'yes' or 'no' or 'maybe' regarding to whether they are important to your work. I'll also give a little bit of feedback what I have already understood from you. *Shaping and influencing organizational communities*, this is something that I think you have been speaking about the whole time, right? So would you agree that it is a big 'yes'?

Stephen: Huge.

Interviewer: *Creating virtual closeness and collaboration spaces* also a big 'yes' for you?

Stephen: Essential.

Interviewer: *Framework setting and mastering technology*, I have also heard that from you a lot of times. *Dealing with complexity* also, definitely. How about *personal branding*?

Stephen: It really is a balance, at times, between position and the human side of you. I think this is addressing it because while there is the deliberate attempt I make to be as human and as accessible as possible, at times there is the role that I have to play, which requires me to be the chief administrative officer. And you have to make sure that in that role, you are always protecting the title. So you just find some ways of doing that to keep that clear, without ever making it a burden. One thing I have not mentioned is that I try to get to each of the offices on a semi-annual basis. And that is again for the obvious reason, that the human contact is very important. I will time it with an audit, a year's end or something other. That is one of those opportunities where I get to play the role because I am coming in for a particular purpose.

Interviewer: That nicely blends into another element we have identified, *contextual leadership*.

Stephen: This is, I think particularly important, the tremendous variations: understanding what is cultural and how to adapt to that. I have identified two or three different cultural styles that I have to pay particular attention to because I have been surprised in the past. And I will be going in a particular vein and all of a sudden I realize, something is spinning terribly out of control and I have no point of reference as to how could this possibly be going wrong. What could possibly be happening here? And 90 percent of the time, if not more, what has happened is, there is a misreading of a cultural norm. And that has caught me off-guard. I have witnessed this with also other people, and one of my roles in the organization is actually watching out for that. We have a new representative from Kazakhstan. He is the first Kazak we have had in the office and it is interesting just to try identifying the cultural patterns that I need to understand here. I have to just basically then keep within those parameters. Perhaps at a later time, as we get to know each other, those boundaries will shift, but right now, there is a certain degree of formality that is in his mind right now and I have to deal with that and respect that and work with that. Completely different when I get to the office in Jakarta, where I am dealing with my representative who is Singaporean. It is a very different environment. Then when I go to Addis Ababa, the representative there is Eritrean, again a very different context. In an international global context I think that customizing leadership has to take into account sensitivity to culture being an important factor.

Interviewer: What about feedback? *Creating a culture where people can exchange feedback*, even across cultures?

Stephen: We have some unique aspects here in terms of the way our religious community functions. There is a process that all Baha'is try to practise, which is referred to in our internal jargon as consultation. And it is a reflective process. And it is one where the whole approach of how you handle issues in the community is you try to be frank and honest and put things on the table when you have an issue and to get engagement of all the parties. An important part of this is listening to the other person. And this is just part of our culture as a religious community, where that kind of feedback is encouraged. My job is to see that this process is present in our professional and organizational context and not just present in the religious part of the community. And that gives me a bit of leverage because I can always go back to that point of reference with people: "Wait a minute. Let us just put this on the table. Let us approach this through consultation." And that instantly says to them, we are going to put a feedback loop in place here and you are going to be safe.

Interviewer: Stephen, as a last element – is *measuring success* important in your leadership practice?

Stephen: That has elements for those people outside of the representational side of the office. My entire professional life has always been on that side of the equation and I have worked in sales organizations, in fund raising organizations, various types of organizations in different points in time. In a sales organization, the salesman is the demigod, right? All attention, all honour flows to the salesman. And you can see that in an advocacy organization, all attention flows to the representative, that person who coordinates that coupe of some sort. So the question becomes, what happens to all those people behind the scenes? Where are their successes? When dealing with my staff, I am frequently using theatrical metaphors. This whole idea of a stage and that we are here making sure that the performance goes off well. And then, as you are dealing with your background people, your aides, your technology people, your financial people, it is about really making sure that they recognize their role in what just happened out there on the stage. One of the places where we will do that is in our regular staff meeting because at staff meetings I always make sure that the representatives are reporting back to the staff and I highlight certain things that are accomplishments that they have achieved. They also have an opportunity to ask some questions to the representatives and engage with them. It just brings them closer. But you have to make sure the measuring of success comes down to that operational level. You have to make sure it moves past them and finds a way to incorporate and engage everybody.

Interviewer: Stephen, your sharing has been really informative and rich. It has been an absolute pleasure, thank you so much for your time.

Stephen: Thank you for giving me this opportunity and good luck with your book.

Interview with Leandro Baghdadi: Start-up inside the machine

Figure 3.2: Leandro Baghdadi's complexity image

Name: Leandro Baghdadi

Age: 34

Family: married, no kids

Employment history: Joined as an intern and spent on average two years in each position: junior assistant, then senior assistant, then coordinator, manager and now Director of External Communications.

Current Position: Responsible for external communications for Latin America and the Caribbean at Ericsson, dealing with 40 markets, working with a team spread all over the region, including direct employees and also third parties. Has been with Ericsson for 15 years.

Interviewer: Approximately how many members does your team have?

Leandro: Today I have six people directly working with me. Four of them work with third parties that are agencies. In each agency there are at least two more people so it is in total around ten third parties. I am in Sao Paolo in Brazil and my team is spread in Chile, Mexico and Costa Rica. We are part of a global organization so I also have that dotted line to Stockholm where the headquarters of Ericsson is. In external communications we handle basically five types of activities, so we are organized into five areas and one function.

Interviewer: Could you share a bit about the complexity that you move through as a leader?

Leandro: The main complexity for me is the size of the region, the amount of markets that we have to handle. In 2010 we decided to restructure into regions. We organized into mainly three groups called tier one, tier two and tier three. Tier one is formed of the most important countries: Brazil, Mexico, Argentina, Colombia and Chile. These five countries are measured by our KPIs, so we have strong KPIs that are most focused on these five countries. Then we have a second group like Ecuador, Peru, Venezuela, Uruguay and mostly countries in South America. Lastly, we have the third group; Central America and Caribbean and this prioritization for sure considers also our function, communications. This was the first way to handle the complexity in the region, how to prioritize countries not only businesswise but also for our function and communications. Based on this decision we started to consider resource allocation where we would have people from the team and in those places where we do not have team members, we need to have third party support. In Colombia, for example, we have a local agency that supports all our efforts. The same is true for Argentina, where we have a big office but we do not have anyone from communications sitting in Argentina. Due to this decision we had many internal complaints, because some people in Argentina or Colombia wanted to have someone providing local support. Communications goes from company strategy to supporting the personal relationship with customers, so people want someone from communications to provide the immediate support. This is still hard to handle because we continue to have these kinds of issues.

Interviewer: Leandro, just a brief question, could it be that this is already a conflict between the organizational models of Family and Machine?

Leandro: I think we have these kinds of conflicts among all three of the models you describe all the time. We have to deal with a lot of headquarters' demands and at the same time you have to consider country needs but then we are organized into a region.

Interviewer: Any other layers of complexity you can describe for us? Are there also some intercultural elements involved? In Latin America there are huge differences between countries and regions. How do you deal with them?

Leandro: It goes from the culture and from language. We think that almost every part of the country speaks Spanish but it is a very different Spanish so it is not that easy to handle. Then we have different time zones so we also have to deal with that. We also have in Latin America something very specific, a particular "sense of urgency". I had some episodes where I thought that the direction I gave to the team or to an individual was very clear but then when you are waiting for something to be delivered, then you realize that it was not so clear.

Interviewer: Was that language challenge? Was it a communication challenge? Was it a challenge regarding push or pull strategies?

Leandro: I think all of them happen and it is amazing how complex that is to handle. One good example is the weekly calls with the whole team. We do not only have people from Latin America, but also an American on the team.

Interviewer: Where is she located?

Leandro: She is based in Costa Rica and she's been there for ten years but she still has to improve her Spanish. Therefore in our weekly calls you can speak in the language you want, either English or Spanish – not Portuguese. At the same time you give freedom for people to make it clear for others to improve their skills on language to understand. For sure this has been the best way so far, since it is important for people to be comfortable when speaking. Then I try to communicate with the team not only by calls but also through the internal messenger because I think text is easier to understand and you can go back to the phrase and read it again and try to understand it in detail.

Interviewer: Do you choose different strategies there in order to engage people in that urgency? Do you see a difference in dotted lines?

Leandro: It is hard to define a specific recipe for that. I think it depends on the kind of people. Some are very engaged or very result-oriented so then it is easier. We are talking about the average of people in the business environment and it is good. We do not want to have these kinds of challenges but for sure when we do I would love to have people all over my team engaged and hungry for results. I think since 2010 we increased the aspect of the results orientation so we connected the KPIs with the personal benefits and rewards. I would say we went to a different level into the relationship manager theme.

Interviewer: So what else forms part of your complexity? One thing I have already heard is obviously that you are communicating a lot virtually. How does that affect the overall complexity?

Leandro: We are not part of the direct business – we are not sales or pre-sales or delivery. Then we have a cost control on trips. So we meet physically, the whole team about every two years. So basically we do 99% of the communication then, and that is for the whole communications team – we are divided in three areas so that's not easy. At the same time this organization that I also have, and also the other areas we have to support including internal customers, are sometimes not sitting in the same place as the person in the communications team, so virtual communication is something that we have to handle with the team, with internal customers, with the whole organization. I think Ericsson has passed through this change since 2010 on a regional perspective and I have people that I talk to almost every day and I do not know personally; I never met physically. But I think it is the trend.

Interviewer: So if you look at that, what does that mean to you as a leader? What has worked well? You gave an example of using chat or messaging for example. What has worked well for you in terms of media and media usage or anything that comes to mind?

Leandro: I think there are two important aspects. The first one is that you have to be available as a leader and this availability is something not that easy. For sure we have different tools to be in touch with people but you have to understand which tool that person prefers and in which tool that person is more effective. The person that works with me sits in Chile, she prefers to talk over the phone. I prefer to chat because I think it is easier, faster and we can align small things with a very quick chat but she prefers to call. At the beginning I asked her why she doesn't just send me a message. She said she needs to feel secure and the best way for that is to hear my voice. That is a very good example on how to deal with the personal preferences on communicating.

Interviewer: So you know all personal preferences of your complete team?

Leandro: I would say yes. I have one person joining the team and we had the first conversation yesterday. In this conversation I tried to provide her the full support and I told her that I preferred to keep in touch on a daily basis by chat, by messaging but if she prefers she can give me a call whenever she wants or via WhatsApp, we have a WhatsApp group. So we have different tools and I think I have to understand which tool each one prefers. The second thing is about how to respect the agenda. I think that is very important because we sit here in Sao Paolo and let us say Sao Paolo is the headquarters of the region so fifty metres away we have the desk of the head of the region. So you can imagine how things just come up here; the sense of urgency is much stronger close to the head of the region and to the Vice President of Strategy and the Vice President of Communication. We are around some of the main executives of the region. And then when I have a meeting booked in ten minutes but the head of the region comes to me and says: "Listen let us chat about the next media interview we are going to have tomorrow" – what do I do? It is very hard to deal with this.

Interviewer: What do you do Leandro?

Leandro: If I tell you that I maintain the meeting I would be lying so it is hard. It depends on the urgency of the matter but I try to respect the agenda and bookings most of the time because it is important for people to feel the respect and accountability because at the end when you do not do things from your side it is hard to understand why people are not doing things from their side.

Interviewer: If they are not in the same physical room with you there are a lot of cues missing. If you are running late, which can always happen, does someone else take over the facilitation of the meeting until you join?

Leandro: Yes we do that, we try to not only have myself responsible for handling, or pushing things.

Interviewer: In meetings you rotate roles? Is that something that you do?

Leandro: Exactly. It includes the definition of the meeting agenda. We like to have a standard agenda, some topics that we have to follow up and then this person can bring topics related to his/her own responsibility. Another thing is that we have the vertical and horizontal responsibility. So we have the functional responsibility e.g. there is one person responsible for paid media but she is also responsible for other internal customers. So she is responsible for one specific function but she is also responsible for communications, for one internal customer, a second and a third; so it is a mix of cross-responsibility not only the technical one but also at the single point of contact for an internal customer. So sometimes this person has to handle all the functions that are not only external communication but also internal communication. That is another department and in that way I think it is important for people not to stay only in the technical function but also to experience management capability because in the end you have to deal with projects, with people so it is much more management than technical competence. It is not so easy for a person to understand this type of responsibility and the change; this change also was initiated when we became a region, so it was something new in the initial two years.

Interviewer: Leandro, do you as a leader also develop people?

Leandro: Yes, for sure. I think this example that I just gave you it is one of the most important parts of the development of people in our team. Having this cross-responsibility, not only working in your specialty and your expertise but develop general competencies to be more. So you have to be a technical person and at the same time a generalist to deal with the whole communications demand.

Interviewer: How do you do that?

Leandro: Well I am not sure if it is a technical explanation but these daily chats are very important to make it clear for people. I do not have all the answers but with these daily chats people can understand. If my internal customers are asking for a note in the intranet it is internal communications activity. What should I do? We have the department of internal communications with the whole team specializing in that. The internal customers do not understand that we are only external communications or we are only internal communications. So that is a very good way to practise how we work with the other functions like internal communications. But also we have the formal process of competence development that is in partnership with AGR so in the beginning of the year we define the major competencies to be developed during the year and we prepare a plan. Then we have a mix of activities to be elected by people like web-based courses or specific training and then we have three times per year the career performance conversation. There we define what this person has to do and it is a common decision, it is not something that the manager has to decide. We have to have a conversation and understand what the directions are that we have to give and provide the support to the career path. I think it is important because everyone expects support on career path but it also depends a lot on the people, they have to decide what they want to do.

Interviewer: I am hearing the different formats of machine and family type of organizations a little bit. Since you are such a big fan of messaging, it almost sounds like some sort of internal knowledge community that you have going at all times regarding the chat function. Are all of you connected through chat during the whole working day?

Leandro: Yes. It's about the availability. We are connected all the time but of course we have meetings and considering the different time zones we start our work two or three hours earlier the local time and it ends another two or three hours after so I think it is not only to be connected but also be available.

Interviewer: We have identified some major elements that we think are part of the complexity that leaders go through and that could be potential initiatives that also leaders take. I would like to read them to you one by one and you could very quickly say yes that is an issue for me, no that is not an issue for me. If you want to give one or two sentences on how you deal with these we appreciate it but you do not need to.

Leandro: Okay.

Interviewer: Shaping and influencing organizational communities.

Leandro: Yes, I think that's very important for me.

Interviewer: Creating work for closeness and collaboration spaces?

Leandro: Totally, 100% – very, very important and very hard to do and you have to re-think all the time.

Interviewer: Framework setting and mastering technology.

Leandro: I think it is important but as a basis, not as a priority.

Interviewer: Dealing with complexity, you've already said yes a lot of times. Personal branding?

Leandro: Yes, that is very, very important and especially for us as a support area. We need to not only deliver but also make the perception of what we have delivered clear. It is about doing but also about being perceived.

Interviewer: If you deal with a lot of entities, which do not share the same physical space with you and if you constantly need to deal with organizations with different organizational paradigms, it could be that you are a different leader in headquarters than you appear to be in Sweden and appear to be in Costa Rica. So obviously that's a question of who are you and how do you come across? This is also something we mean by personal branding. Do you do something where people would say, regardless of which type of organization they sit in or regardless of which culture they sit in, this is Leandro and you are aware of this? Have you actively developed the sort of image of yourself?

Leandro: Especially with Ericsson because we have a very, very global organization, we are in 180 countries and there is a lot of opportunity for rotation. But when you decide to leave your country to go to another position in another country, then it depends a lot on how well you are perceived not only on the person that will hire you but also on the whole communication of the organization globally. As a head of external communication I am very exposed to the perception of the global head of communications including the CEO for example, so yes is very important for you to work with the perception of yourself and how others perceive you. We have this kind of structured process of feedback – three hundred sixty feedback – so we get the feedback from our peers, we get feedback from our bosses, from our teams, from people. You can just choose anyone that you want to have feedback from and then you can send this person a questionnaire and then you receive his or her feedback because it is very hard to evaluate yourself. It is very important even though it's not very nice all the time. Some people are tough, some people are very honest or some people are just a good friend of you but you have to deal with these differences to understand how you are really perceived by the whole community.

Interviewer: How about contextual leadership, are you adapting your leadership style to various circumstances?

Leandro: Especially to personal circumstances. A person in my team for example, had a kid and then had some issues with the kid on the school and then the person needed some flexibility to leave the office sometimes to handle the situation. I think it is important to understand that and when you understand and you provide this time for the person, then it is easier and very rewarding when this person can be a hundred percent available and dedicated. For sure this person will be more efficient than ever so I think it is important because in the end we are human so we have to understand that sometimes a person doesn't have a good day.

Interviewer: Creating a culture of feedback. In feedback we do not mean 360 degree or any sort of ritualized feedback but unofficial feedback.

Leandro: I think it is very important but I think we have to be careful with providing feedback all the time because it is not that easy to be in that person's shoes so it is easy to have an opinion, an immediate opinion. You should wait a little bit to understand what happened and especially if it is a negative feedback. You have to really understand why something happened, how it could be done differently. It is important to be careful because it is easy to express opinions but not that easy to act upon.

Interviewer: Absolutely. Last but not least, measuring and celebrating success.

Leandro: Yes that is really important, especially when you have a virtual organization, where you do not have the proper time to celebrate. You have to try to define ways of celebrating. When we do our weekly calls and we have very good news in terms of results I try to start the meeting by that topic and especially to make the whole meeting lighter so we start talking and laughing. I think that's very important and you need to try to do that on a regular basis. Sometimes you also have to mix the structural way to have mechanisms of rewarding but you also have to consider the "thank you" as the very basic thing.

Interviewer: Leandro thank you so much. Any closing words that you have for the readers, anything that comes to mind?

Leandro: Well I think we can stay here talking for hours about how to deal with people because it is not easy but it is very, very rewarding. I used to work with one or two people, now I have a bigger group of people that I have daily conversations with, also with the people in the agencies and the same time with the teams. So when we see an evaluation, when we see good results, I think it is very rewarding to see that we can work together mutually and we can deal with the challenge. That is very, very rewarding.

Interviewer: Leandro thank you so much.

Leandro: Thank you. Very, very, very nice to be in this work with you and good luck.

Interview with Patricia Anthony:
As we go faster and faster

Figure 3.3: Patricia Anthony's complexity image

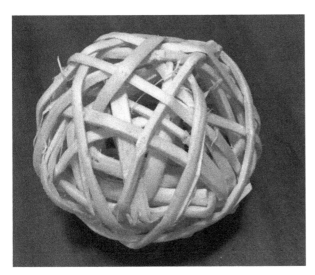

Name: Patricia Anthony

Nationality: US-American, grew up in Turkey and the Netherlands

Family Status: Single

Education: Registered dietician by profession

Job history:

- Nutrition support for people who cannot eat/not eat normally since 30 years

- 2000–2012: Working for Nestlé in the world head-quarters in Switzerland with a lot of time spent in Asia and Europe

Current position: Leader of Medical Affairs Team at Fresenius

Interviewer: Welcome, Patricia. Could you share the virtual, organizational and probably also cultural complexity you are moving through as well as what your main tasks as a leader are at Fresenius?

Patricia: I work a lot in international contexts. We are leading the US medical team, but as we are trying to bring new products to the US the actual project managers for the projects are based in either Germany or Sweden. My morning is basically encompassed with conference calls, trying to talk to those in Germany; trying to help people understand what is needed in the US. We deal a fair amount with the FDA (Federal Drug Administration), trying to help people understand how our standards differ from what they are used to. I would say that a good 50 percent of my day is dealing with people of multiple nationalities be it German, French, Swedish and go from there. We are lucky that they all speak superb English; the language is not a barrier, but there are definitely challenges as to how people understand what is being requested of them and how we approach problems, and when it comes down to the regulatory side it can get very sticky. I think that is a challenge. Working for a German company now I notice the cultural changes more than before when I lived in Europe. Before it was more French or more international I think. So you had French people, you had Australians, you had some Germans, you had Americans, but it was a little bit more blended. So I think sometimes we – as nationalities – do have certain characteristics but sometimes when we are melded into a group some of those aid a little bit more, whereas working with a true German company, the German part really becomes a little stronger. I also see that sometimes the formality of the European culture stands out versus the Americans. I know we are seen as kind of bulldozing things through. But sometimes that requires sensitivity on both sides, so as to not offend and to understand. I think when you talk about hyper-complexity the challenge is that people are moving so fast and trying to do so much and relying so much on technology that they don't listen. They take some time to listen, but they hear a little bit more what they want to hear and I think our ultimate communication is not as good as it was. I am a very, very big proponent of picking up the telephone and not sending five emails. I think email is a good way to document something and, obviously, a good way to communicate, but I think we rely on it too much and we end up in very sticky situations because people interpret the tone as they feel it and not as it was meant and people also respond too quickly and thus do not read it carefully. I am always saying with my team, stop... do not send another email just pick up the phone. As much as we can get done via WebEx, via email and so on, I do not think we are ever going to replace the need for some face-to-face and getting to know the people as a person.

Interviewer: How big is your team; how many report to you directly and how many dotted lines do you have?

Patricia: Well, my team is in the process of growing so right now I have two direct reports and one dotted line. Actually, I would say two dotted lines and I am adding another three more people, so that will be this year and there is a possibility to add another four next year. So, as we grow our business here, I grow my team.

Interviewer: As a leader you are facing intercultural, communication and also media challenges. You are already setting a frame in terms of saying people must not rely on emails but also take other media into account. How do you deal with various organizational paradigms, the ones we describe as "Family", "Machine", and "Network"?

Patricia: I think we very much work in a network. The project team that I work on for many of the projects is spread all over the world. We rely on them for key input but we have no reporting structure. So you have the organizational structure of each business unit, though the market unit of the US is different than the corporate business structure and there is a different culture in each place and you have to deal with that. A huge part of my day-to-day interaction is getting people to do things who do not report to me than those who do report to me. So it is very much relationship building and you have to understand what is important to them and how to position it so that you meet a need. I think that some of the basic sales principles these days people forget is that people want to be valued and people want to know that you know who they are and that they are important. To me that comes into every people interaction whether I am dealing with a physician, a patient or whether I am dealing with a vice-president in Germany where I need their support to help something happen.

Interviewer: You get members to do what you need and what they want through personal recognition and acknowledgement of what they need. Are there other things that you do that work well for you in the network? And are there things that you have tried that did not work at all?

Patricia: I think being highly demanding and saying, "I need this and this is when I need it" does not always help. I think you need to be sensitive to their other demands, being very respectful of people rather than getting frustrated or angry when they do not do something. What you find in Asian cultures – really letting them save their face – is also important in the rest of the world. People do not like to be told, "You are wrong", or, "You did something bad". Sometimes there is nothing you can do, but at least give that person an opportunity. So, I really believe in developing relationships with people and right now I am under a great deal of pressure to get a lot done and I just said to somebody yesterday that even though I am not necessarily always meeting the deadline, for some reason I have some empathy. People are saying, "Oh yes, yes, she has too much on her plate, blah-blah" which kind of surprised me, but I think it is because when people know you are working hard and you are pushing to get it, they are willing to cut you a little bit more slack. But at the same time you have to try to meet their goal and help them. I think the world is all about people and how we can communicate and respect each other and as we go faster and faster you cannot just get mad at somebody because they make a mistake. If we are doing ten things at the same time, as much as we do not like it we are human and we are going to make a mistake.

Interviewer: Do people that you are reporting to have the same patience with you as you with others?

Patricia: Well, I think they have patience with me. It is interesting to hear you say that I have patience because I do not think that it is one of my strengths and people would say that I am very direct. I do not like to leave anything up to interpretation. Some people do say I have patience, but I am often seen as somebody who really pushes things. So do my staff have patience with me? I think, yes in some ways. I think that they see me as a team player and somebody who will stand up for them, someone who's interested in their growth. I think one of the biggest problems in the world we have today is that we have too many people with big egos asking, "What is in it for me?" and I do not believe in that philosophy. If somebody in my team can do something better than me I would like to promote them for it. Maybe they can teach me and I think that in the long run we are going to get somewhere better. So I believe a leader's job is to grow their people and to give them the best opportunities and I think as an outcome overall business or operation will do better. So I am a very, very big proponent of true teamwork, it is more important than what is in it for me.

Interviewer: One of the elements that we think has played a strong role in hyper-complexity is to shape and influence organizational communities. Do you do something like that at Fresenius?

Patricia: I would say we do not have that. It is probably a good idea. I think people are too much task orientated and we do not sit back and smell the roses and see what we could do better.

Interviewer: Another topic we think is important is creating virtual closeness and good spaces in which to collaborate virtually. Is this something that has relevance to you?

Patricia: I think media has its role. But I think that putting all your efforts into one media is a problem. We do tons of phone conferences and they all have a positive role but I still believe for good teams and real collaborations having a few face-to-face meetings periodically really helps to build a team. It is that personal relationship you can build by seeing and being with somebody. Having a meal with them or something tends to be a little bit more effective. We have that with a couple of our projects where we are trying to get information from factory and we are just the Americans over here that just need, need, need. Whereas, if we sit down and talk to them and you actually have time and it is not an hour conference call you can actually say, "This is why I need it. Help me understand" and okay, "So show me what you do? How do I...?" go in and actually seeing their workplace, things like that. I think that breaks down some barriers and we've seen that on our big projects. We try to have one big team meeting in person so that you can understand: this is what we need and this is why. But I believe in media. I think it is the way of the future. We have to do more of it, but I still believe that we are never going to get away from a little bit face-to-face.

Interviewer: How about framework setting? I have the feeling that this is something that you are doing a lot.

Patricia: Yes, I do it a lot. I am not sure it is integrated well into the company. I think it is very important to have agendas and to follow them. If a meeting's for an hour do not routinely have it for an hour and a half because then you impose on other things. You are basically saying to people, time is not important. I think people start to expect that. When I was at Nestlé something that was very clear was that you had an agenda and that the only people that get invited to the meeting are the ones who truly need to be there and it does not mean that other people are not important. What it means is you respected other people's time because if they do not have to be part of that discussion then they have something more important to do. I think people get offended if they do not get invited to a meeting. But it also means that it requires you to build trust in the people who have the responsibility for that aspect.

Interviewer: What about *personal branding* as a leader? Is that a topic that matters to you?

Patricia: I think that I do not know that I have a personal brand. I think that if someone described me, at least I would want them to say that I was honest, straightforward and highly capable. Those are things that I want to note and, you know, somebody who knows what they are doing yet is fair and a team player probably. I never really thought about myself as a brand.

Interviewer: What about *contextual leadership*? Adapting your leadership styles to the different circumstances, do you do that? Do you believe it is important?

Patricia: I think it is very important. It might not be a style but you need to deal with each one of your employees in a different way because what makes them tick is maybe a little different. I think it is basically understanding people that you are talking to and leading in a way that is appropriate for them.

Interviewer: *Creating a culture of feedback*, is that important for you?

Patricia: Absolutely, incredibly important.

Interviewer: And *measuring success*, is that something that you find important as well?

Patricia: Yes, I also believe in measuring and celebrating success, because I think that, you know, people like to say, "Hey, we did this" and sometimes even breaking big projects down into smaller successes. It helps to continue to motivate people because sometimes the overall project can be so overwhelming you do not feel like you are getting anywhere. But, when you can do it in small pieces you can have a lot of successes and I think we all need to feel like we are accomplishing something. I hope we spent enough time and I think in this fast-paced world right now but I do not think we do... we are just moving, moving, moving.

Interviewer: Patricia, thank you so much for the honour of sharing a bit of your time with us.

Interview with Javier Escobedo:
Constantly connected

Figure 3.4: Javier Escobedo's complexity image

Javier spends much of his working time communicating in front of a screen.

Name: Javier Escobedo

Nationality: Mexican, has lived in nine cities on four continents during the last 20 years. Currently living in San Francisco, USA.

Age: 49

Family: Married, with a 15-year-old son and a 12-year-old daughter

Education: Major in Actuarial Sciences, MBA from the University of Chicago, five years of training in the marketing school of Procter & Gamble

Employment history: Has worked in marketing and commercial functions since 1990 in different industries and in different company sizes with a lot of staff responsibility.

Current Position: Global head of marketing and digital sales at a global bank (a major Spanish bank).

Interviewer: Could you describe the global complexity that you are moving through? How big is your team? How many direct and dotted lines do you have? And in general, what does your work look like as a leader in this complexity?

Javier: We just opened up an office and we are probably going to have about 150 employees. Right now, we just have seven people in San Francisco. Think about that – the team is 350 people, 250 people – and none of them are near me. That means I will be on a plane all the time and use systems like WebEx sometimes four, five hours a day. I need to be coordinated; I need to get people to be authentic. To believe in people just through the screen is hard and I need to trust people quite a bit. What helps me to keep the complexity at bay is the quality of the people I hire to make sure that their actions are reasonable. I cannot follow up with everyone in nine time zones. So in a way that simplifies a little bit of the complexity. The other thing is that this bank is about a hundred years old and it has never changed; it has always done the same things. Trying to make it a real digital bank is a big, big challenge. So there is also a lot of complexity in trying to change and really transform the bank. Digital does not necessarily mean web-based any more. Digital just means things happen a lot faster and information travels in different ways, so that is another big challenge of the complexity.

Interviewer: If you have people in so many different time zones and you mostly communicate with them virtually, what specific challenges do you find in communicating virtually?

Javier: The biggest problem we are having right now is that the bank – as we transform it – brings people that are better prepared and have lived in "digital worlds". Few of us are bilingual; the bank is highly Spain-centric. So over the years speaking English has not been a value of people that have been here for a long time. The language barrier is difficult in the sense that I speak both languages, but then I am in meetings where I know that people don't understand the other's language. I just had to navigate that over lunch!

Interviewer: How did you do that?

Javier: Well, I will focus on the language that is the lowest common denominator, or the most disruptive. For instance, one person understands quite a bit of English, but cannot speak it very well, and another does not know any Spanish. I will proceed in English and speak slowly, so that everyone will get it. And there is also a lot of simultaneous interpretation going on. In crucial communication, language is a huge barrier beyond your day-to-day business.

Also in terms of communication: I have been around the block with Europe, the US and Latin America for many, many years, so I kind of know most of their codes, communication, verbal, non-verbal – but not a lot of people do. The bank had traditionally been Spanish, so there was this animosity that the Spanish were the "conquerors," and the other guys felt "conquered" and sceptical. Moving away from onsite command and control is an issue for the Spanish. The other side is to avoid and resist turning into a service organisation that is data driven. That is a whole other problem, but in that respect the communication is really difficult because the communication right now regarding the language is just based on conquest, right? I control you and you report to me, even though you do not officially report to me.

The third out of three complexities in communication is that this bank has been nurturing a culture that avoids conflict. Things are never spoken out; rarely agreements are made; and the fact that somebody nods does not mean, "Yes," – it simply means she is nodding and nothing else. You cannot really count on many things happening, and then there is a lot of blockage. Clearly, the lack of clarity in communication – regardless of the language – is a daily issue in this institution. I deal with that every day.

Interviewer: That is on an organisational cultural level, on a relationship level within the organisation and on a language level. Do you think it is also on an intercultural level?

Javier: I think it starts with intercultural. I think there is very little willingness to really go the extra mile to try to understand the differences in the cultures. That has not been ingrained in the DNA of the bank. The first time they began to join meetings, the [US] Americans were getting to conclusions in two minutes: "Yeah, this looks about right. Let's go." The Spanish were saying, "We have to debate it; hear everybody's opinion." Then, the Spanish were talking for hours and the [US] Americans would just check out. Navigating that is really, really difficult, so I would say it is an intercultural thing. Everything cascades from that. That, and the company culture. So it is not intercultural, it is the way the culture of the bank has evolved over a hundred years.

Interviewer: You have given a wonderful example of how you handle some of the complexity in a virtual context. Do you have more examples where you would say: "There I tried something, or I handled something successfully that really works for me?"

Javier: You live, you learn, like the saying goes. Over the years, I have moved into a value-add management style.

Especially when you are a change agent, you are coming into all these different roles all the time; you need to prove yourself. I mean, a gift is a gift in any language, so I have driven my team to just not make a lot of false promises until we can actually deliver something. And that has worked well as a bridge across language. Of course, the definition of "success" and the definition of "delivery" and the balance between the how and the what are very different among cultures. Yet, I think that is not the biggest problem here. Everybody will value an accomplishment and I think that is a big advantage.

The other thing, which is a very current topic and in everybody's mouth through the work, is being data-driven. Particularly in a culture like a bank or like an e-commerce company, just managing the data and having a focus on generating data for decision-making and discussion has been an issue before in terms of building solid credibility. I have gotten into two types of situations. After a couple of experiences in things that needed to be turned around – which I liked when I was younger – I decided that I must work on things that are growing and that have a lot of potential. The other thing is that I have focused on things that I know how to do. That makes my job somewhat easier.

Interviewer: If you think about these three different organisational paradigms that I described in the beginning – family, machine and network – can you recognise them in your work challenges? If so, how do you deal with that?

Javier: The family thing is exactly what I was telling you in the lack of confidence. Naturally, with a family, you will be hierarchical and Dad will say: "I am Dad, whatever you want. So you better pay attention and you better behave." They show a little bit of an unconditional relationship here in that they will love you regardless of what you do. The supposedly variable compensation is like three percent, so it is not that much and it is fairly steady.

Then there is a ton of people who have been here for years and years – 15 years, 10, 20 years. There is a guy I met who has been with the bank for 42 years because he started as an intern when he was in high school. In the beginning, I thought this must be a great place to work – which it is – but the only reason you stay is because you just do what you are supposed to do: Show up for work every morning; type up your little thing that you do every day. Just get it done with enough quality, and you will be rewarded with a job for life with very little variance in the income. That was the model then. So that is a little like family. I might take my son's allowance a couple of times, but really, he can do no wrong. I mean, I will love him regardless, right?

The second one was the machine. Well, this thing is a huge machine. I mean, we have 120,000 people, and more than 2,000 offices in all the farthest places. And they all work very similarly. They have pretty much the same procedures. Unfortunately, every single bank in the world has the same thing. They all love the same. We all look like dollar coins, but there is very little differentiation, so we are like the products of a machine. When you have an organization this size, you really cannot question authority or question direction. You just got to move on because if everyone in the middle or lower ranks asked one question, you would have 120,000 questions to answer, or 100,000 questions to answer. That would be really, really hard.

Interviewer: You have children that ask their father questions and then you have 120,000 questions that cannot be answered at once. That itself seems to be a little contradiction. How do you deal with that?

Javier: I do not manage the long tail, so I do not manage a 15,000-person organisation, which changes everything.

The discipline that those guys must have and what they are focused on is all about the bigger numbers and how they roll up. They have to deal with exceptions in a certain way. This is not my situation. I feel that my group has always been closer to machine working.

So the third one was network. We are all remote. We all talk to each other. There is no hierarchy. I encourage, and have had people from all levels of my organisation, respond to me and just send me an email, or just say "Hi" in the hallway.

But going back to the question: How do you manage the complexity of the machine? The worst that can happen to a machine is downtime. When you are working in an operations world, the worst thing that can happen is downtime. The absolute worst thing is unplanned downtime. What you want is to have consistency in the operation, and then optimisation towards that. That is exactly how it works. When you can work in an even flow and just keep people operating, it really moves pretty well. Particularly in a Latin American culture, people will tell you: "Yeah, it will be ready tomorrow. I am working on it. It will be finished soon. Soon you will get it." "Mañana, mañana," just means not today; it is the only thing it means. The way I manage that is to make sure the machine is producing what it is supposed to output. I do not generally try to change the machine to a network. I am doing this very rigorous review of work every week. They tell me it's crazy, but if they can't produce for me what they are working on, it means they are not doing enough, and that the machine is just not working the way it should be working.

Interviewer: How about the network? The network is voluntary. How do you get people to deliver who you have no direct disciplinary control over?

Javier: I am just learning these steps of the organisation.

It used to be very hierarchical in the past, and I am just getting to the point in which it is all very flat. I did some personal experiments in my agency start-up, the company I had for six years in New York, in which we were organised completely differently. We had a little bit of hierarchy, but there was really in no fixed salary. It was all variable and we were organised in a way that there was open seating with no assigned desks. People did not have to come to the office if they did not want to and, everyone was connected very loosely. What happens in a network is that it is very fluid and unpredictable in a sense. It is almost contradictory to a machine. A machine will produce things at regular intervals with whatever widget it is designed to produce, but a network has billions of different possibilities of outcomes and anything can happen. Managing that network requires you to deal with people in a way that is non-linear and have a situation in which you can have the communication flow in the way it's needed. You just have to have that network deliver what they need to deliver at the end, and then you have got to trust the system and make sure that this thing works. Trust the process. The network is very loose and people will be very creative, but they have a very defined process that they follow. And that will result in good things that make sense. It needs a little bit of process and management of that non-linear form of communication.

Interviewer: If you could put a number to it roughly in terms of leading, what would say: How much do you need to lead or how much can you lead in a family type of organisational setting? How much in a machine and how much in a network?

Javier: That is really interesting. At the end of the day in a family or a network organisation, it is all about the example you give and how you behave. When it is a machine, you are more in the role of an operator of the machine. When the machine is working well, you just press "On" or "Off," depending on how many levels you manage. You do not need to behave; the machine is just going to work. The higher you go up in the organisation, the more time you spent leading and giving directions. When I am on a trip, I will spend 10 to 14 hours a day speaking with people. So I devote about 20 percent of my time when I am back home just to speak with my directors, which I do every week. And I spent an enormous amount of time to speak with people in the network and the family. In this bank I am not running a machine. I am running more of a start-up kind of business. So, that is how I deal with it – a little bit of process, and a little bit of example. Ultimately, it all goes back to the process that includes a leadership and an example skill.

Interviewer: I have some central parameters that I just want to throw out at you and you can very briefly say, "Yes," you think it's important in dealing with the complexity that you are moving through, or not. Is it important or is it an essential element in dealing with the complexity that you are moving through to shape and to influence organisational communities.

Javier: The thing is, shape and influence are two very different things. You do not always have the opportunity to shape, particularly when it is a machine, but influencing is definitely an important piece. Most of us are really going to bring that complexity into work or into something that we find manageable. So it depends on your listening competence and your leadership style. We are all going to have to use influence. I would answer: half and half.

Interviewer: Creating virtual closeness and collaboration spaces?

Javier: Very important. And collaboration spaces don't necessarily mean a place, a meeting room. There are days when I will spend five hours in video conferences, so that my ears hurt after five hours with headphones, but it is incredibly important.

Interviewer: Framework setting and mastering technology?

Javier: I think it depends on the complexity. If I have everybody in the same room, the technology is probably not necessary. So I have to give you the worst answer in the world: It just depends. As to the first part of the question: When I talk about process, I mean frameworks. We have a weekly review in which each of my team members are going to have their half-hour with me. Even if I didn't answer their emails for five days, they know that they are going to see me in the next couple of days. All that rhythm brings some method to the madness. So yes, I would say incredibly important.

Interviewer: Personal branding?

Javier: Personal branding is important because of the people you are able to attract. When you want to get chaos into order – depending on the complexity of the chaos – you are going to need people to really help out. You need to be able to track the right kind of leaders; people who will really come and work for you or with you. So, people will be checking out your LinkedIn page; they will be Googling; and they are going to ask your friends about you. If they find out that you are a leader who screams at people, they are not going to work there, even if it's the best company in the world.

Interviewer: Contextual leadership?

Javier: It's like adapting the frameworks. I think it's really, really important. You have the frameworks and you just have to know when to use them.

Interviewer: Creating a culture of feedback?

Javier: Super, super important. Easier said than done. There are some places where it will just not happen and you will just have to get rid of the people that do not have the tendency to provide standard feedback. And there is the opposite of that. You would think the opposite of giving feedback is giving no feedback, but for me the opposite of giving feedback is talking behind people's backs. That is the opposite, because no feedback is just zero. So if feedback is one, no feedback is zero. But minus one is just talking – not talking directly about things. As much as I think feedback is important, when there is a backchannel communication and things do not get communicated in the right way in the right place because there is no openness for whatever reason, that minus one will kill you. You will start losing people. So that is a big issue.

Interviewer: Last one would be measuring success and also celebrating it.

Javier: And compensating for it. I come from a world that is so finely tuned, that there is very little that an operator can do to change the output, except turn on the machine. If you turn it on, it is going to work. There is no knob. You are not going to be able to increase output by two percent or whatever, unless you use the idea of highly differentiating compensation as a way to really drive the right behaviours. I use a couple of frameworks there and many are getting you more analysis than you wanted, but it is the only way. You have got to analyse all your positions, you have A players in A positions and then B players in B positions, and so on and so forth. Person A in position B will get bored and leery. Have B people in A positions and they will screw up in business and screw up the whole organisation, no matter their position. And then the other ones are overcompensated stars. So there has got to be an understanding of who is doing a really, really good job, by whatever means you define a really good job. So for me, the compensation fees are as important as everything else.

Interviewer: Javier, thank you so much, this has been extremely informative.

Javier: I hope it helps. I have all these frameworks in my head, I hope I did not put your frameworks into my frameworks too much.

Interviewer: No, no, no.

Javier: Okay, I have been doing it for such a long time, you know, managing in a certain way.

Interviewer: No worries, there was a lot of good information in there for the reader. So, thank you so much.

Part IV: Deeper into the mix

Introduction

This chapter is dedicated to those readers who love to get more insights into the theoretical reasoning that is behind the content of this book and to people who want to be inspired by new but still fragile approaches in the field of communication, leadership and coaching.

We also have included some key concepts from our book "Closeness at Distance: Leading Virtual Groups to High Performance"[*] to give access to some basic concepts that we have developed further in this book with respect to the leadership perspective and the purpose orientation of global networks and communities. However we still suggest going back to the original book if you want to get to know the practical aspects of global collaboration and high performance.

There is no real logical order of the different elements of this chapter – each one is a little raw diamond that is attractive on its own. Raw in the sense that one can devote a whole book on any of these little contributions but we thought it is also an added value to give you some insight on our new development and reasoning that are

---

[*]   Hildebrandt et al. (2013).

the building blocks for our future new approaches and products.

This chapter is also meant as a catalyst to start a dialogue and joint research with us on these new and inspiring topics.

The concepts of complexity and hyper-complexity

In our age, we often say that something is really complex and that we have to reduce complexity. To shed light on the meaning and workings of complexity, we would like to offer you some insights from physics[*].

Let's start by drawing the lines between "something is complicated", "something is complex" and "something is chaotic".

A system is complicated when

- it consists of many subsystems;

- it is possible to deduce all characteristic features of the system as a whole from the characteristic features of the subsystem and the interaction of both;

- it is possible to precisely describe the state the system and its subsystems are in;

- the future development of the system is predictable in the long run.

A system is complex when

- it is not possible to deduce all characteristic features of the system as a whole from the characteristic

---

[*]   Richter, Rost (2004).

features of the subsystems and the interaction of both. The system is more than the sum of its subsystems with emerging pattern formation;

- it is in principle not possible to precisely describe the state the system and its subsystems are in and, as a consequence of that,

- the future development of the system is not predictable in the long run.

A system is chaotic when

- small changes in the system can lead to large changes in the system (butterfly effect);

- the future development of the system is not predictable in the long run.

When trying to model complex and chaotic systems, physicists have found that it's not easy to precisely describe the notion of complexity. Phenomenological approaches that try to classify different degrees of complexity just by the apparent pattern of behaviours displayed by complex systems (self-similarity, strange attractors, etc.) are in certain contexts not able to distinguish between chaotic and complex systems.

That's why scientists made the following distinction. The degree of a system's complexity can be described by the complexity of its behaviour or appearance (Apparent Complexity) and/or by the amount of information needed to "construct" and thus "copy" the system (Algorithmic Complexity). It follows that while complex and chaotic systems may have the same degree of complexity in appearance, complex systems may be much more difficult to be simulated or copied/reconstructed artificially compared to chaotic systems: It is obvious that the information content of an anthill with all its individual interactions and the resulting patterns is much higher than that of a Mandelbrot set of fractals which can be created by a very easy computer algorithm[*].

For those who do not know what a Mandelbrot set is: imagine an equilateral triangle. Now, imagine smaller equilateral triangles perched in the centre of each side of the original triangle – you have a Star of David. Now, place still smaller equilateral triangles in the centre of each of the star's 12 sides. Repeat this process infinitely and you have a Koch snowflake, a mind-bending geometric figure with an infinitely large perimeter, yet with a finite area.

Let's now turn to the concept of "hyper-complexity", which, in our opinion, best describes contemporary work environments, especially those of global network organizations.

We know from mathematics that different degrees of infinity exist, for example countable infinite (the set of integral numbers is countable infinite: 1,2,3,4, etc.) and uncountable infinite (the continuum of numbers between 0 and 1, including hyper-real numbers, is uncountable infinite). We coined "hyper-complexity" to describe this uncountable degree of complexity.

Or consider hypertext on the Internet. Due to the links between different documents it is in principle not possible to map the knowledge of the Internet in a two-dimensional item such as a book. In our early Internet pioneer days a group of us jointly wrote a book online, called "eLearning and eCooperation"[†], using a software similar to a Wiki (Wiki didn't exist yet then). The publisher desperately tried to convert this text into a book format, ignoring our appeals to make the virtual text accessible on a CD.

---

[*]   Mandelbrot (2010).
[†]   Glatt et al. (2002).

And we see the same effect in our context: social complexity is linked with dynamic complexity is linked with market complexity is linked with...

The concepts of groups, networks and communities

If we have a larger group of people, let's say more than ten people who partly interact with each other, two new characteristic traits arise within this larger group: the network aspect and the community aspect. These are described by Wenger[*] as follows:

- The **network** aspect refers to the set of relationships, personal interactions, and connections among participants, viewed as a set of nodes and links, with its affordances for information flows and helpful linkages.

- The **community** aspect refers to the development of a shared identity around a topic that represents a collective intention – however tacit and distributed – to steward a domain of knowledge and to sustain learning about it.

Depending on the purpose and context, one of the two aspects can be so strong that we can classify this group as a community or a social network.

In this case, according to Michael Wu[†], the main differences between these two constellations can be described as follows.

Social networks are:

- Held together by *pre-established* interpersonal

---

[*] Wenger (1998).

[†] http://community.lithium.com/t5/Science-of-Social-blog/Community-vs-Social-Network/ba-p/5283.

relationships between individuals. So you know everyone that is directly connected to you.

• Each person has one social network. But a person can have different social graphs depending on what relationship we want to focus on.

• They have a network structure.

Figure 4.1: Structure of a social network that extends around the whole globe

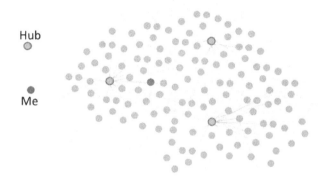

Communities are:

• Held together by some common interests of a large group of people. Although there may be pre-existing interpersonal relationships between members of a community, this is not required. So new members usually don't know most of the people in the community.

• Any one person may be part of many communities.

• They have an overlapping and nested structure.

Figure 4.2: The structure of a community is usually hierarchical, nested and overlapping. And each person is usually part of many communities at any given time.

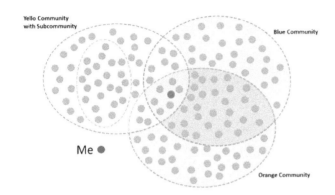

In our daily work we have to deal with hybrid situations, where we have structures that are partly team like but also have network and community elements.

The following factors will help you determine in what kind of structure you are:

- Importance of project management in the group.

- Importance of identity of the group.

- Degree of cultural diversity.

- Degree of virtualization within the group.

- Mixture of internal, semi-internals (contracted people) and externals.

Figure 4.3: Which structure do you work in?

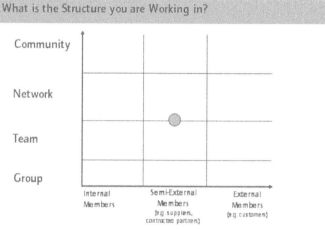

Exhibit 4.1: Example: Hybrid team and network structure in the automotive industry

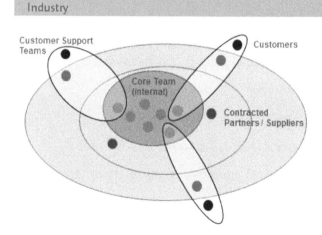

The most important features of social networks

If one wants to influence a social network or a community or desires to innovate, one has to focus on two important features of these social structures:

- Hubs, and

* Weak links.

Figure 4.4: Central elements of social networks

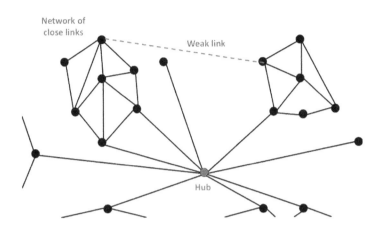

Hubs are knots within networks or communities that basically everybody is connected with. They are the places, people or institutions in which the main streams of information come together or have their origin.

Weak links play an important role in problem solving. People tend to look for solutions to their problems in their networks they are most familiar with. However, these networks are characterized by the very fact that the members share a lot of things and in most cases also mental models. Taking this into account, it is quite unlikely to get radically new insights on existing problems by sharing them with people who are alike. One should rather think of not so established links to networks or communities that strongly differ from the ones in which one is most. Activating these "weak links" to other networked structures is key to creating innovation and solving problems.

Community Development and Dynamics

In spite of being a large group and an open system the dynamics of a community in its life cycle show similar patterns to those displayed by small groups in their development:

- Forming

- Storming

- Norming

- Performing

- Adjourning/Transforming.

However, being an open system, a community needs a certain critical mass of members to reach the state of storming after the initial kick-off. If there is no exponential or really large and fast growth, the community is perceived as not "lively".

Basically the **90-9-1 rule** describes the degree of liveliness within a community in a natural and average situation that reaches the critical point of growth. Given 100 members, 90 of them never contribute but might read what has been posted within the community, nine of them sometimes contribute and one member is continuously active.

As an example, in a community of 1,000 members one can only expect ten members to contribute on a continuous basis.

The maximum rate of growth takes place in the storming phase and turns to a turning point at the end of the norming phase, the time in which the community consolidates its conduct of behaviour and rituals and enters the performance phase. In that phase, the investment into the community can be harvested which then reaches a point where growth comes to an end, the number of members decreases and "newbies" entering the scene balance each other.

Exhibit 4.2: Community life cycle

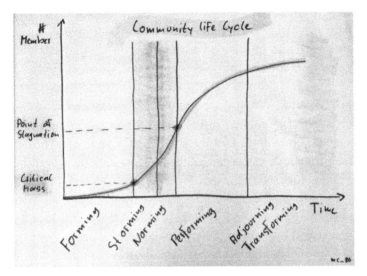

Amy Jo Kim* was a pioneer in describing what is needed to successfully master the first phases of a successful community.

It needs attractive (virtual) spaces that are technically suited to meet the intended purpose of the community. Successful communities are polarizing on all levels: wording, colours, pictures, structure, technical features, etc. You either love or hate it.

The most important asset of communities is its set of members. It is therefore essential that the community allow for dynamic user profiles. For example, we want to see with one mouse click what a person has posted and in which contexts a person is involved or how I am linked to this person.

---

*   Kim (2006).

In the phase of large growth one has to create roles and codes of conduct within the community. This should go hand in hand with honouring members who have added special value to the community and who have served as role models by giving them visibility, new roles and privileges with higher responsibility. This provides more structure and guidance within the growing network and helps to guide the purpose which people identify with.

In the same direction point initiatives to create cyclic events and rituals within the community – to celebrate the best contribution of the month, to host an all member meeting once per year, to have a special on boarding process for new members, etc.

Sustained growth can only be reached if the community starts to show self-similarity in its growing parts. For this one has to allow for self-organized subgroups and skilled community managers that went through a community leadership training programme.

Figure 4.5: Community development

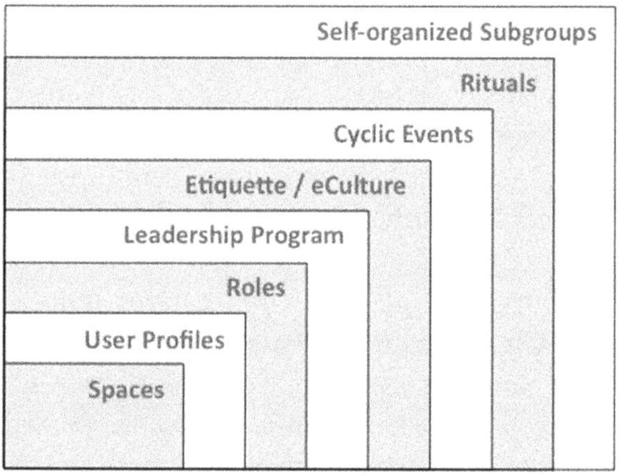

```
Self-organized Subgroups
    Rituals
    Cyclic Events
  Etiquette / eCulture
  Leadership Program
      Roles
  User Profiles
    Spaces
```

Amy Jo Kim

Some remarks about Generation Y

Which challenges are posed by Generation Y, who have entered the world of work, to corporate management? How can you cope with these challenges in the globally connected world?

We believe the answer is: connect! Create the feeling of being connected.

While Generation Y is very self-conscious, having a sense of belonging and an anchor is very important to them. Our concepts of virtual closeness and the modern world of work reflect this need.

Generation Y

- grew up, often as sole children, in a society that focused on its children. These are therefore very self-confident and need constant recognition.

- know that the resource of time is limited which is why they want to hit the ground running. The failure to make substantial use of their time and giving them tasks that are perceived as meaningless lead to discord and impatience.

- value purposeful communication. In order to help the company be successful they want to know where they are positioned. Generation Y demands, unlike previous generations, regular feedback from supervisors. "I want to be seen."

- go for power, fun and meaning in working life. They want to have a successful career as much as they want a fulfilled private life. They demand the possibility of combining work, family and leisure – work-life-blend.

- are "digital natives" and because of their affinity for technology, they are an advantage for companies.

Members of Generation Y want to have an innovative workplace with state-of-the-art equipment. From their point of view, smartphones and laptops are necessary to meet accessibility and rapidity. They will only stay on when they feel that they belong to something meaningful. That's why leaders need to create a feeling of belonging.

Some remarks about situational and contextual leadership

The basis of situational leadership, as introduced by Paul Hersey and Ken Blanchard[*], is the conviction that for a given task an employee has to perform, the leadership situation is characterized by the commitment and the competence of the employee in focus. Depending on this leadership situation, the manager can adjust her approach towards the employee within a two-dimensional intervention portfolio with directive or supportive behaviour as the two axes. Thus situational leadership is a great example of customizing your leadership initiatives towards each individual under your guidance.

Situational leadership's main areas of application are family-like contexts and partly also machine-like environments such as a matrix organization with clearer concepts of roles and responsibilities.

In networks or community-like structures, the basis of situational leadership no longer holds to its full extent. The concept of tasks and roles is partially overwritten by the notions of identity and purpose (see chapter "Contextual leadership", p. 93) as the work to be performed is too complex and changing too fast. In most cases it is not possible to break down the work into tasks attributed to individuals. The competences of the individual members of the group are needed in a dynamic and interdependent

---

[*]   Hersey, Blanchard (1969).

but not always predictable manner. "Act first, then analyze" replaces the traditional concept of "think first, then act".

As a consequence, traditional planning and project management break down to a certain extent. Rather, it's analyzing the context, then acting, then analyzing again and adjusting in the situation. Network leaders must be able to deal with the unknown and to be in touch with their intuition. A clear sign of this is the advent of new approaches in the field of project management, specifically the SCRUM method as an example for agile project management and lean development.

Further, directive leadership approaches are difficult, if not impossible, to apply in virtual and networked groups. In most cases, one has to lead along "dotted lines", not having direct reports. Or one's direct reports are out of sight in another time zone thousands of kilometres away.

In spite of situational leadership's failure in networks, the main idea of customizing one's leadership approach to the individuals one guides, remains a valid and success-critical idea. Refer to chapter "Contextual leadership", p. 93, to see how this can be done.

Here we are focusing on the paradigm shift to replace the concept of "situation" by the concept of "context" and its practical consequences.

As the interdependence of the different group members is so high and interactions are so dynamic, leaders need to take the full picture into account because an isolated situational view of the individual is not really helpful. The full picture includes the following aspects.

- One part of the context is made up by the overall framework, i.e. the global space for collaboration with all its technical and cultural aspects.

- The other comes from the individuals' needs and competences, i.e. the identities of the different group members.

- Last, but not least, it also consists of the purpose of global collaboration.

- The perception and therefore the analysis of this context is coloured by one's own cultural background.

These facets define the context in which an employee is embedded. We call the corresponding approach of customized leadership **contextual leadership.** Contextual leadership speaks to hyper-complexity in that it emphasizes both the macroscopic framework and overall purpose of collaborating as well as the microscopic level of identities and their interactions, both face-to-face and virtually.

Situational leadership is guided by the role and the task the person who is being led carries out. Remember the characteristics of family- and machine-type organizations from Part I? Especially in the machine, roles and tasks define its complexity and guide management efforts to reduce this complexity. Roles and tasks are clearly predefined, and the people who carry them out are deemed exchangeable, at least on systems' level. The context a leader must be able to navigate is determined by clearly defined roles and tasks and the corresponding parameters for success. Leading based on those roles and tasks is therefore appropriate and useful.

In the network, however, it is no longer the roles and tasks alone that define the context. It is the person that is more important and more visible in the network organization than the role or task itself that might be very fuzzy and spread out over the whole network. The demand for individual initiative, innovation and entrepreneurial spirit characterize the global network organization with its unprecedented level of organizational complexity. To understand the network, a leader must study the context of those he or she leads in order to cope with the complexity of situations.

See chapter "Contextual leadership", p. 93, for more on this.

Identifying and applying our inner resources to complex decision-making

Laurence Baltzer and Marcus Hildebrandt conducted action research and a lot of personal introspection over nearly two years to come up with a model of the brain. Based on the results, they combined existing tools and developed new ones in order to support managers to use the potential of their unconscious mind for improved and sustained decision-making.

On the way they realized that some of the really relevant information that we as human beings can access, at least in principle, is nearly chronically neglected in complex problem solving and decision-making.

Here is their schematic model for the brain in the context of decision-making in complex environments.

Figure 4.6: Decision-making model

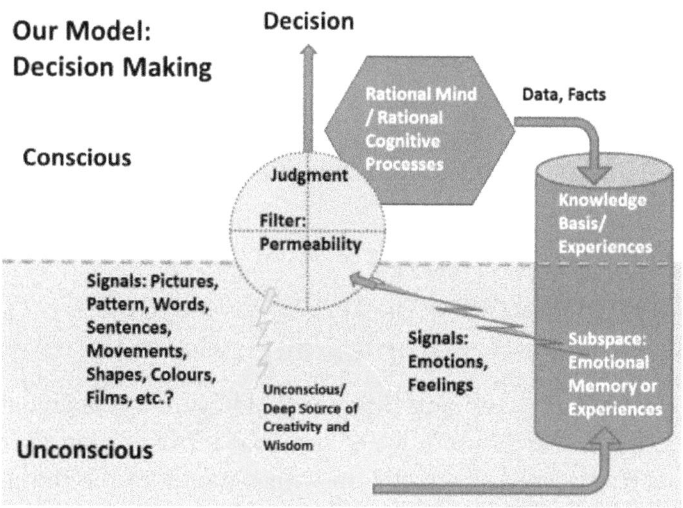

In the following, we use computer terminology whenever possible to explain the model.

The model basically consists of the hardware and the software people use for problem solving. Part of the software is static and implemented in the hardware, while another part of the software is dynamic and created based on the needs and demands of the context in which we move. Correspondingly, the hardware is partly static and partly dynamically created during the process of learning.

The most important part of our hardware is our database where we store knowledge and experiences as data and facts. In living beings from a certain evolutional level onwards, all entries into their database are connected to the emotions they were feeling when the knowledge was created. Another distinguishing factor for living beings is the degree to which they have access to the database on a conscious level and the degree to which data are only used unconsciously.

In decision-making, the following distinction must be

made carefully. Does a decision we have to make show similarities to past contexts or not?

Let's first assume that our current context or our desired future context (decisions are usually linked to future states we want to achieve) is similar to a context in our past. In this case, the brain and body, automatically and immediately, realize this much faster than we could ever possibly think it through rationally. This automatic recognition process registers the full complexity of the situation. The brain compares whole "pictures or films" of current or future situations with already existing/experienced/stored situations of the past.

In fact, this is the secret of search engines. They don't search but rather, they compare index systems of databases that are constantly expanded. This is much faster than scanning the whole Internet for the subject of the search.

If a match is found, there is a mechanism – similar to an analogous digital converter – that checks the (former/old) emotion attached to this context (the decision that was made in the past). If the emotion is pleasant and positive, the system creates a body signal that says, "Yes, I want this, go for it." If the emotion is unpleasant and negative, the body signals, "No, I don't want this, avoid it."

These signals are called somatic markers (see Maja Storch[*] for further information on this). These somatic markers differ from human being to human being. Some of us get a clumsy feeling in the stomach, others feel pressure in the chest, to mention just two typical negative somatic markers. Positive ones may include a tingling sensation in the stomach and the feeling of warm energy flooding the body.

---

[*]   Storch (2012).

Knowing your own somatic markers and being able to detect them in complex decision-making processes is a major success factor. Some people call this "gut decisions". However, these decisions have to be checked rationally. Real "good" decisions feel good and make sense from a rational point of view.

Unfortunately, we carry inside of us filters created by our biography and by cultural standards that might prevent us from connecting to the body's wisdom and taking it seriously. These filters may even prevent us from detecting these body signals in the first place.

But how can we deal with contexts to which we can't apply any past experiences? Here we partly enter new ground, practically and theoretically. We believe that it is not only rational thoughts and emotions that determine us and also a lot of animals but there is also something else that might distinguish us from most of the animals: We know from our own introspection and from talking to others that there is a dynamic system in our mind which we call the deep source of creativity and wisdom.

Figure 4.7: Conscious and unconscious mind

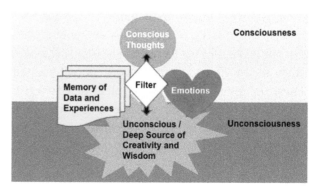

You are not only your thoughts...
You are not only your emotions....
You are more!

Maybe you have experienced the following phenomenon. One day you suddenly get the idea for dealing with a problem. Or you suddenly realize a mistake you made. And you just know and feel that your idea is true and must be acted upon. These experiences often happen in the absence of stress and during moments and in environments that allow us to relax deeply, perhaps while jogging, taking a bath, drinking a glass of wine, hiking, waking up, laying wide awake at night, meditating, etc.

The information we receive in these moments is often called intuition.

We believe that this should be distinguished from the notion of heuristics, which describes a set of "rules of thumb" based on past experience in the context of repeating patterns. Intuition, on the other hand, is a singular mental event in response to an unprecedented context.

Some people have learned how to stimulate this deep source in favour of their needs, using their intuition to identify possible answers to pressing questions. Others can draw on their intuition to generate ideas but may not use it further than this. Yet other people get surprised when these moments happen "accidentally". Finally, a number of people only have access to this deep source while dreaming during the day or night.

Figure 4.8: Different degrees of maturity

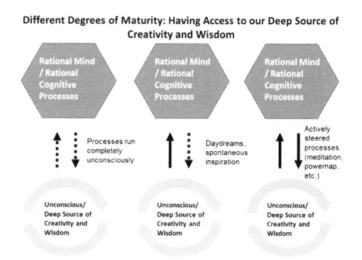

We believe that one can learn to find increasing and increasingly deliberate access to this resource. Mindfulness provides great methods to achieve this.

Some final postulates about the deep source of creativity and wisdom every human being carries inside themselves.

- It works 24/7.

- Rational thinking processes and critical emotional states take priority over this mode of problem solving and suppress access to this source.

- It always provides the "best" solution in any given context and its boundary conditions, which are set by the information you feed into the dynamic system and have stored in your knowledge database.

Principles of communication and their connection to network and community dynamics

Paul Watzlawick created five basic rules (pragmatic axioms) that seek to explain human communication and its inherent paradoxes[*]:

1. It is not possible to not communicate.

2. Every act of communication carries an aspect of content and an aspect of relationship.

3. Communication is always cause and effect.

4. Human communication uses analogue and digital modalities.

5. Communication is either symmetric or complementary.

Marshall McLuhan added to this set another pragmatically based axiom:

The medium is the message.[†]

McLuhan assumed that not the transmitted content of a medium but the characteristics of the medium itself have an impact on society in which the medium acts. In the 1960s, he also anticipated the emergence of global interaction spaces in the context of globalization and introduced the concept of the "global village".

Our concept of the purple space is going in the same direction but differs insofar as the creation of a purple space is an intentional act of leadership and not merely an emerging pattern in society.

---

[*] http://www.paulwatzlawick.de/axiome.html.

[†] McLuhan (1964).

Based on, and possibly in generalization of, the axioms posited by Paul Watzlawick and Marshall McLuhan as well as the principles of organizational development introduced by Niklas Luhmann[*] and Karl E. Weick[†] (every organization is formed and stabilized by a shared identity/ sense making), we postulate the following seven axioms that describe our practical experiences of communication and network dynamics.

1. Every human being can attribute to a relationship between him or her and another individual or another more abstract object of relationship (e.g. an organization, a process, an artificial intelligence, etc.) a degree of virtual closeness (virtual distance).

2. Every communication can be associated with an (online) identity (social presence, cognitive presence and leadership presence).

3. Every communication has an impact on the degree of virtual closeness – there is no neutral communication. The absence of communication is a special form of communication.

4. Communication is influenced by the real or anticipated response to the communication.

5. Communication that allows positive sense making for the receiver is attractive and increases the feeling of virtual closeness.

6. Acts of communication that appreciate the differences/the diversity (e.g. attitudes, behaviours, etc.) among cooperating communication members lead to an increase of virtual closeness between the group members and are therefore the basis for high performance within this set of members.

---

[*] Luhmann (1987).
[†] Weick (2015).

7. The quality of acts of communication between different group members (and therefore the corresponding online identities and the corresponding network of virtual closeness), shared communication media and a shared communication purpose define a framework in which purple spaces (e.g. global, attractive cooperation spaces of reduced communication complexity) can emerge or be created.

Any leadership intervention is based on communication. Therefore, in order to make an impact with one's own communication processes we suggest taking these seven axioms into account when planning the intervention.

Feedback in international contexts: results from our research

Between 2011 and 2014, Marcus Hildebrandt and Stefan Meister conducted a research project about international feedback culture. The objective of the research was twofold:

1. to detect cultural differences and similarities in giving and receiving feedback, and

2. to identify main factors to model personal preferences of giving and receiving feedback in an international context.

The sole focus of the research was on situations related to spontaneous, work-related feedback. It did not ask about formalized feedback such as annual performance appraisals. See chapter "Shaping global dialogue", p. 159, for the model of Resonant Feedback that was developed based on this research.

Background and respondents' profiles

This research project was inspired by the fact that little systematic research exists about the concept of feedback and personal feedback preferences across cultures. While much knowledge has been accumulated about feedback on the one hand and the influence of culture on feedback on the other, there seems to be no systematic study of feedback preferences across cultures.

The findings of this study shed light on possible areas of improvement of feedback cultures in internationally operating organizations, whose members often work in cross-cultural teams and are tasked with developing feedback models that work for all members. Additionally, it enables individuals or teams working at specific cultural interfaces to adapt their feedback to potential local practices.

In a survey sent to professionals across the world, they asked questions related to situations of spontaneous, work-related feedback in country-relevant professional contexts. This meant they concentrated on companies that mainly work with a local workforce. 50 to 75 datasets were received from professionals whose organizations operate in countries including Brazil, China, Germany, India, Mexico, Russia, and the USA.

Exhibit 4.3: Nationality

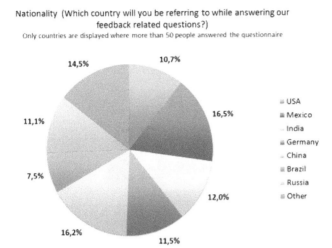

Nationality (Which country will you be referring to while answering our feedback related questions?)

Only countries are displayed where more than 50 people answered the questionnaire

Slightly more than half of the respondents were male.

Exhibit 4.4: Gender

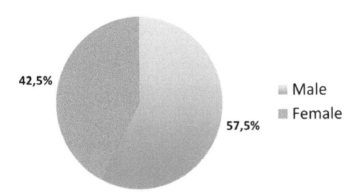

With nearly two-thirds, the majority of participants work in human resources. Other professional fields include the following industries: automotive, education management, financial services, IT, management consulting, marketing and sales, media production and PR.

The three most represented age groups among the respondents were 30–39, 20–29, and 40–49 years. This suggests a range from young to very experienced professionals.

Exhibit 4.5: Age

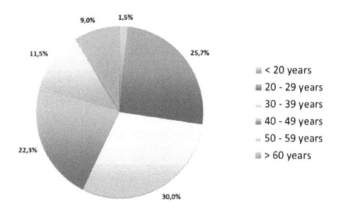

Finally, when asked about the length of their current employment, one-third responded less than two years, close to one-third responded two to five years, and slightly more than 20% each responded five to nine years and more than ten years respectively.

Exhibit 4.6: Length of employment

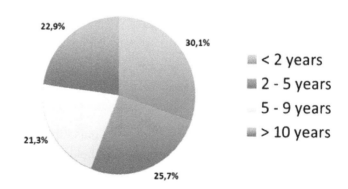

Findings

Which factors most influence giving and receiving feedback?

Respondents considered the following three factors as most significant (in order of weight): professional expertise, professional hierarchy, and length of employment. Age, gender, and ethnicity received significantly lower responses.

When is feedback most valuable?

Across all respondent cultures, feedback was regarded as most valuable when the feedback giver has higher professional expertise, stands higher up in the professional hierarchy and has more work experience than the receiver. Gender and ethnicity, on the other hand, has the least impact on the perceived value of feedback.

Identity of the person providing the feedback: peers or superiors?

In the majority of cases, feedback is given both by peers and by superiors.

Feedback from peers

Among peers, respondents' general preference is receiving feedback from people they feel close to. In many cases, these are also the actual feedback givers. Chinese respondents had the highest preference for getting feedback from peers who they feel distant from, directly followed by Germans and Mexicans.

Feedback subject: performance or personal development?

The most prominent feedback subject among respondents was their performance, meaning the completion of tasks in work-related processes, behaviour related to goal achievement or leadership behaviour. While almost all respondents indicated that they'd prefer feedback that is related to both performance and personal development (the latter meaning the improvement of personal skills), far more than all other responding cultures the Russians indicated that they'd prefer to receive feedback related to their performance.

Feedback style: explicit or implicit?

When asked about explicit and implicit feedback, almost all respondents indicated that the observations of feedback are mostly both, with the exception of China, where feedback tended to be mostly explicit. Indian respondents declared the highest amount (100%) of implicit feedback and the lowest preference for receiving explicit feedback. All other respondents expressed a high preference for explicit feedback, with Russia and the USA leading the list.

Feedback timing: when is feedback given after the respective situation?

The time when respondents receive feedback after the respective situation varied greatly. While Russians, Germans and Chinese indicated that they mostly receive feedback immediately, US American respondents mostly receive feedback a few days later. Indians made equal indications for immediate feedback, feedback that comes a few hours after the situation and feedback that follows a few days later. The highest incidents of receiving feedback a few weeks to months after the fact were indicated by Chinese respondents.

Feedback place and setting: formal or informal?

Respondents were asked to indicate whether the feedback setting was rather formal or rather informal. Perhaps surprisingly, feedback happens overwhelmingly in formal places with formal settings for all respondents.

Feedback audience: is feedback given in the presence of one's group?

In the overwhelming majority, feedback is mostly given to respondents on a one-on-one basis in the absence of the groups they belong to. In China, feedback is nearly equally often given in the presence of one's group, both as individual and collective feedback. The clear preference across all respondent cultures is for one-on-one feedback.

Feedback medium: face-to-face or via technology?

The overwhelming majority of respondents indicated their preference for face-to-face feedback, with all responses ranking between a 70 and 100% preference.

Feedback media

When feedback can't be provided face-to-face, however, the most common media employed for giving feedback by far include email and telephone. Videoconference ranks surprisingly low. Social media and instant messaging are predominantly used in China. Telephone and email also rank as the two highest preferences for feedback through media.

Some concepts from "Closeness at a Distance" *

a) Virtual Closeness

After working with virtual groups for more than a decade, we felt we were, in a modest way, successful in our efforts; but we would nevertheless hit limits. This often happened in two areas:

- The clients' realities were growing so complex that they often required half a day or more of precious face-to-face time to understand and map out their processes and networks.

- Even when we had succeeded in disentangling their landscapes of collaboration, clients often wanted everything at once from a workshop and it was thus hard to satisfy all their demands.

In short, we had the feeling we were lacking precision in face of increasing complexity. As these experiences were accumulating, we decided it was time to do something about it. For two years we researched and evaluated our own experiences and also those of others, drawing from contact with and learning from the pioneers in the field: Jessica Lipnack, Jeffrey Stamps, and Karen Sobel Lojesky.

Our breakthrough came when we realized that there was indeed one unifying success criteria for all virtual teams, groups, and networks: the degree of perceived "closeness" felt towards the group, the project/process, the stakeholders, and/or the organization involved – Virtual Closeness. Virtual Closeness lies at the core of our approach to working with virtual groups.

---

* Taken from Hildebrandt et al. (2013), p. 3 ff; see also the pioneering work of Lipnack; Stamps (2000); Lojesky; Reilly (2008).

Virtual Closeness describes the perceived closeness between two or more group members and their perceived closeness to the context and space wherein they interact (what we chose to call "Purple Space") after a period of little or no face-to-face contact.

What makes the concept of Virtual Closeness unique is that it doesn't only refer to people feeling close to each other. It also implies that people feel close to the spaces wherein they communicate and collaborate and to the mental objects that represent the virtual work environment such as processes and structures. This understanding of closeness is crucial in late modernity when globalization and advanced technology have created new and rather intangible virtual interaction spaces. Especially in business environments, these virtual spaces – as a critical success factor for high performance – need to be even more attractive than the virtual spaces that are visited outside of working time. Taking care of the building blocks of Virtual Closeness helps virtual groups to create a unique and shared identity and a feeling of belonging and immersion in these spaces and the organization wherein the space is embedded.

b) Virtual Performance Assessment (VPA) at a Glance

Making virtual collaboration work is a continuous process of improving group performance. The Virtual Performance Assessment (VPA) is designed to do exactly that. Informed by our experience of working with virtual teams, groups, and networks, our aim has been to develop a hands-on, pragmatic toolbox of great practical use to the daily reality of virtual groups.

VPA is a systemic approach to working with any unit of an organization and with the whole range of organizational stakeholders: senior managers, line managers, teams, groups, and networks. Holistic by design, VPA mirrors the systemic complexity of virtual groups. It integrates all organizational dimensions including relationships, the factual, and the organizational. In its comprehensiveness, VPA exceeds all other existing virtual performance improvement approaches, which mainly intervene on the group level, media or technology and tend to ignore vital aspects such as the organizational embedding.

The VPA framework consists of five categories wherein Virtual Closeness can be built and performance improved: Inclusion; Organization and Process; Space and Time; E-Culture; and Members, Tasks, and Objectives.

Introduction to VPA Categories and Dimensions

Figure 4.9: VPA categories

To map virtual performance and provide the basis for Purple Spaces, we have developed a comprehensive assessment tool, the Virtual Performance Assessment (VPA). VPA maps virtual performance in twenty dimensions grouped into five categories.

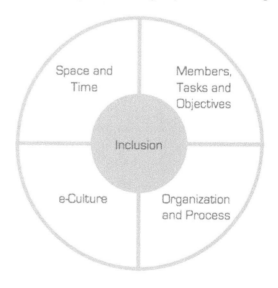

c) Media and communication processes[*]

Synchronous and Asynchronous Media

Marginalizing asynchronous tools such as blogs, wikis, or discussion forums, many organizations follow a constant trend towards more synchronous tools including VOIP (e.g. Skype), SMS, micro blogging (e.g. Twitter), or email on mobile phones. Communication processes are increasingly accelerated by the fast-growing use of synchronous media. This is complemented by a growth in the use of more integrated communication systems. It has become good practice to run a chat parallel to a telephone conference in order to record meeting minutes instantly (a great support for non-native English speakers or groups facing language issues). Likewise, application sharing during videoconferences has been established as an effective tool to focus on documents discussed online.

Divergent and Convergent Communication Processes

Most communication processes can be categorized as divergent or convergent. In divergent processes, the communicator seeks out the different existing opinions, ideas, and perspectives on dealing with a given context, thereby increasing the amount of relevant information as much as possible. In convergent communication, on the other hand, the objective is to reach a point of conclusion, to come to a decision, to summarize, or to solve a conflict. The amount of relevant information is decreased as far as possible.

---

[*]   Ibid., chapter 8.

Figure 4.10: Divergent and convergent communication processes

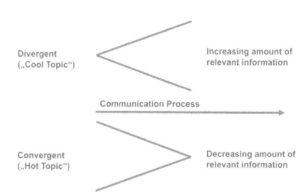

The more time people have to think about options, new ideas, and solutions to challenges, the higher the quality and quantity of collected information will be. On the other hand, if people want to make a decision (when all options are on the table and clear to everyone and the decision-makers are on board and involved) this is best done synchronously. The reason is that in synchronous communication, others' immediate reactions can be perceived and reacted to accordingly, thereby speeding up the decision-making process. These observations lead to a rule of thumb about the match of communication processes and media.

Text box 4.1: Asynchronous media are great for ...

- Asynchronous media are great for divergent communication processes.
- Synchronous media are great for convergent communication processes.

A typical example of divergent communication is brainstorming. The quality of results of a brainstorming process is increased if participants have sufficient time to think about their own ideas as well as the others' contributions. Being able to brainstorm for about a week using asynchronous media like a discussion forum, a blog, or a wiki, a group is very likely to come up with better results than during an hour of face-to-face idea production.

This is especially true when cultural aspects are of concern. In some cultures, people are reluctant to come up with ideas in face-to-face encounters because they may feel exposed to the group and at risk of losing face. This is different in the virtual world. Asynchronous online brainstorming is therefore a culturally sensible solution in addition to promising better overall results. Another advantage of asynchronous text-based work is that it helps overcome language barriers more easily as people can take the time they need to translate and think about contributions.

Finally, if a group environment allows posting contributions anonymously, the full potential of brainstorming can be realized.

Anonymity can also be useful in certain synchronous settings. Using electronic group decision-making or feedback instruments may increase the honesty and authenticity of feedback and decisions. When employees are asked for input or feedback on a decision, results usually differ significantly depending on whether they are expected to voice their opinions in front of colleagues and managers or allowed to present their views anonymously in a virtual space.

While the asynchronous world is the realm of creative and divergent processes, synchronous communication is best suited for soliciting immediate responses, including non-verbal reactions. This allows refining the outcomes of a communication process step by step in real time, but at the cost of reducing the degree of freedom for coming up with a better solution, decision, or joint statement or summary.

Figure 4.11: Synchronous and asynchronous media in convergent and divergent communication processes

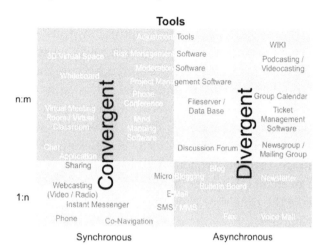

The two tables below contain suggestions on how to use different media in different communication situations.

Table 4.1: Purpose, media and synchronicity

Communication Situation	Media	Synchronous / Asynchronous
Getting to know each other	F2F, Chat, Forum	Both
Asking questions	F2F, Telephone, E-Mail, Chat, IM, Forum	Both
Solving conflict	F2F	Synchronous
Negotiating	F2F, Telephone, Video-conference, Telephone conference	Synchronous
Exchanging confidential information	F2F, (IM, SMS), Telephone	Synchronous
Taking decisions	F2F, Chat, Video-conference, Telephone conference	Synchronous
Brainstorming	Forum, F2F Tool	Both
Informing	E-Mail, WIKI	Push or Pull-Strategy
Keeping in contact	Telephone, E-Mail, Chat, IM, SMS	Both
Distributing information quickly	Telephone, Video-confer-ence, IM, SMS	Synchronous

Table 4.2: Media and purpose

Media	Communication Situation
F2F	Getting to know each other/ Solving conflicts/ Negotiating/Exchanging information/ Making decisions
E-Mail	Informing / Asking questions / Keeping in contact
Telephone	Asking Questions / Keeping in contact/ Quickly distributing information/ Exchanging confidential information
Telephone conference, Video-conference	Getting to know each other/ Negotiating/ Making decisions/ Quickly distributing information
Chat	Keeping in contact/ Getting to know each other/ Asking questions
Forum	Asking questions/ Getting to know each other/ Brainstorming
WIKI	Informing/ Getting to know each other/ Asking questions
IM	Keeping in contact/ Asking questions/ Quickly distributing information
SMS	Keeping in contact /Asking questions/ Quickly distributing information

Formal and Informal Communication Processes

Communication processes can further be classified as formal and informal. Certain media like instant messaging are better suited for informal communication than others. Providing and managing formal as well as informal interaction spaces is an important success factor for leading groups in a virtual and intercultural context to high performance.

In collective cultures, for example, it is important for virtual participants to regularly consult within the home group before and after a decision, and during a brainstorming session or ongoing discussion to ensure social norms such as hierarchies are respected. It is therefore necessary (and good practice) to allow for informal breaks during virtual meetings or for instant messaging or chatting processes to take place simultaneously. While this particularly applies to participants from collective cultures, it could be good practice in any event. After all, people from more individualist cultures often also underlie certain hierarchical restrictions, which force them to check in with their home fronts on a regular basis.

Figure 4.12: Formal and informal communication settings

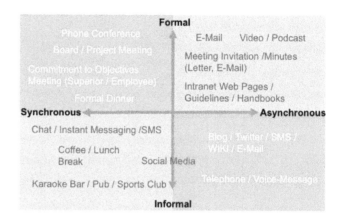

Online identity*

Text box 4.2: Indicators for cognitive presence

Indicators for cognitive presence include the following actions in the communicative routine of a virtual group:
- Problems and surprises are expressed
- Information is exchanged
- Suggestions are made
- Brainstorming takes place
- Syntheses are suggested
- Summaries are made
- Applications are discussed
- Insight is gained from arguments and conflict

---

* Ibid., chapter 8.

Text box 4.3: Social presence in a telephone conference

In a phone conference, social presence can be created with the following measures:

- Start a telephone conference with a round of human-interest stories, which can be designed in a number of ways. One example includes every member sharing a statement about his or her current personal or professional situation. Or members could share gossip about what's going on in their respective locations. The point is to start with an exchange of informal rather than formal information in order to warm up. What is everyone's current context, including cultural aspects such as holidays? What's the weather like?
- End with rounds of members giving each other feedback, on what has been presented during the meeting or on other current work.
- Structure a meeting and simulate reality by using a team clock and/or avatars. If 3D technology isn't available yet, having the images of members' avatars visible for everyone is a good way of creating social presence.
- Don't present substantial data and facts during a teleconference – they can be read before or after. Do, however, market the data and information that demand action. Offer data to catch the others' attention.
- Use storytelling to promote data and facts, for example with success stories.

Text box 4.4: Indicators for leadership presence

A wide spread leadership task in virtuality is e-moderation or e-coaching. Typical indicators for leadership presence marshaled by the moderator or coach include:

- Identifying areas of agreement / discourse
- Seeking to reach consensus / fostering understanding
- Encouraging, acknowledging, or reinforcing team contributions
- Setting a climate for learning
- Drawing in participants, promoting discussion
- Assessing process efficiency

New approaches to coaching: Immersive Coaching

Hyper-complex contexts not only create new challenges for leaders and ask for new leadership approaches but also have an impact on those systems that support leaders in doing their job in a most professional way.

- It is very difficult for managers to make appointments with their coaches face-to-face in a regular and predictable order. In most cases when immediate support is needed there are no appointments available.

- Further, as we have already stressed more than once, it is important to be embedded in the context when dealing with complex situations.

In learning, a new approach has emerged that is called immersive learning. Immersive learning provides answers to these challenges[*].

Since we perceive coaching as a learning format that is best suited for upper management, we have been exploring how this concept of immersive learning can be translated into eCoaching.

Line Jehle and Marcus Hildebrandt have been working on this for years. They managed successfully to transfer peer group consulting and the critical incident method (see chapter "Shaping global dialogue", p. 159) to the virtual world using virtual classrooms or web conference systems. They have also created and followed up on different approaches.

Line Jehle is focusing on embedding the young or more experienced leaders in a learning environment using

---

[*]   Pagano (2014).

simulations and role play, even hiring actors for role play, in virtual classrooms and web conferencing systems. In one of these programmes – the so-called Management Accelerator at eBay, participants have to simulate a project as leaders and team players (alternating roles) and then deal with complex situations. There is basically no input given. All participants learn from each other and from peer and coach feedback.

Marcus Hildebrandt, a pioneer of using three-dimensional worlds*, tries to achieve this effect of immersion by using three-dimensional virtual worlds. Together with Laurence Baltzer and Katja Kantelberg, he has developed the concept of immersive coaching*†.

Exhibit 4.7: Immersive coaching

Immersive means in this context:

- The coach and the coachee meet in a three-dimensional virtual coaching world as avatars.

- The coaching may take place in a specific learning situation that resembles reality.

---

* Hildebrandt, Gässler (2001).

† www.immersive-coaching.com.

- The coaching process consists of a continuum of synchronous, possibly spontaneous meetings as well as asynchronous interaction between meetings.

While developing this concept, we realized that the role of the coaching space itself is in most cases underestimated and the positive potential that the design of the space can have on coaching events is not realized. Upon checking the coaching spaces of our colleagues, we realized that the design of the coaching space was more of a personal state-ment of the coach rather than creating a design that puts the coachee and their development objectives into focus.

Here is an example of our quality criteria for a coaching space that is best suited for the starting phase of a coaching process (static setting), face-to-face or virtually.

Objectives:

One should create a functional space that sparks a certain feeling of "warmth" and "being protected". At the same time, it should create the notion of "timelessness" and thus promote a deceleration from the hectic pace of daily business. Also, it should be clear by the very architecture and design of the space that this room is focused on the coachee and their development goals. Best would be a dedicated space that remains in exactly the same configu-ration as it was left after the first session.

Central (virtual) elements:

- Borders/ Surfaces:
    - As working areas
    - To visualize results
    - Element of wellness (borders)
    - To place objects
- Elements to sit on
- Catering elements (Social function)

- Learning/coaching materials

- Light (warmth)

- Acoustics (protection/closeness)

Another success factor for providing any kind of eCoaching is virtual closeness. You can apply the 20 dimensions of virtual closeness* to the concept of coaching by translating the dimensions in the following way (Marcus Hildebrandt©):

- Space and Time (this corresponds to the new concept of an immersive coaching space and the notion of timelessness and deceleration)

- Time investment
  - How is the time fit/duration time for the synchronous coaching sessions?
  - Is there enough time for the coachee to prepare and debrief between the synchronous sessions?

- Time in shared dialogue (synchronous eCoaching)
  - Does the session promote the feeling of timelessness and the perception of deceleration?
  - Does the coachee achieve a kind of flow-state/how is the intensity of the eCoaching process?

- Work – schedule overlap (integration in the daily work context):
  - What happens in the time between the synchronous interactions? Are asynchronous eCoaching elements available?
  - Is a self-paced eCoaching rhythm possible (flexible time windows/availability of coach, response times)?

---

* Hildebrandt et al. (2013).

- Geographic advantage = eCoaching space
  - Is the eCoaching space a dedicated space and tailored to the needs and development goals of the coachee?
  - Does the space promote the feeling of being protected and wellbeing? Does the space promote the feeling of being immersed?

- e-Culture

- Media competence
  - Are technological entrance barriers low? Is it user friendly (intuitive user interface)?
  - Are the media used suited to achieve the different eCoaching objectives?

- Shared netiquette (accepted from both sides and reducing complexity)
  - Is there an agreement on how to use the different tools?
  - Is there an agreement on response times, etc.?

- Online Identity of the coach (to be seen or not to be seen is the question)
  - How is the social presence?
  - How is the cognitive presence?
  - How is the leadership presence?

- Are there positive experiences from virtual collaboration/eCoaching prior to the eCoaching process (digital online socialization)?

- Inclusion (eCoaching style in an intercultural context)

- Do the working styles and the corresponding expectations fit?

- Do the communication styles and the corresponding expectations (push/pull) fit?

- How is shared leadership implemented (leading and pacing, self-organization, etc.)?

- Is there a shared and resonant feedback and voicing culture?

- Organization und Process (organization and process of eCoaching)

- Access to information and power (knowledge management)
  - Is all information that is relevant to the eCoaching process as well as results from the process always up to date and available?
  - Is it possible to access the eCoaching platform 24/7?
  - Is the coach always up to date?

- Workflow integration (eCoaching solution)
  - Is there a seamless interplay between the different eCoaching steps and elements?
  - Is there an integrated platform in which all eCoaching steps and elements can be realized, supported and documented?

- Organizational relevance (relevance of eCoaching)
  - Is the eCoaching relevant for the coachee?
  - Is the eCoaching and the corresponding development goals of the coachee relevant to their environment/the stakeholders/sponsors/the organization?
  - Does the coachee have experiences of success that are seen by external people? Is there a successful learning transfer into the organization?
  - Does the coachee have enough self-organization skills (self-management)?
  - Is there a development goal oriented pull behaviour with respect to the competences of the coach?
  - Are there efforts to prepare and follow-up on the synchronous meetings from both sides?

- People, tasks and objectives (contracting on fact and relationship level)

- Language skills
  - Does the coachee have the conviction to be able to express and formulate all relevant content in working language?
  - Does the coach use a language that is easy to understand?

- Quality of relationships
  - Is there a good relationship and/or pre-trust between coach and coachee even before the eCoaching starts?
  - Is there a good and trustworthy relationship between the two coaching partners during the eCoaching process?

- Information sharing
  - Is there a good and pro-active information flow in both directions?

- Identification with group and objectives (identification with the eCoaching process)
  - What are the results of the contracting process (clear objectives, roles and responsibilities, expectation management)?
  - Do both partners identify with the objectives and the process of eCoaching?
  - Does the coachee have the feeling that they and their needs are in the focus of the eCoaching (should also apply to the coach!)?

References

Albert, R., H. Jeong, A.-L. Barabási (2000) Error and attack tolerance of complex networks. Nature 406, 378–382.

Flanagan, J.C. (1954) Critical Incidents. Psychological Bulletin.

Garrison, D.R., T. Anderson, W. Archer (2000) Critical Inquiry in a Text-Based Environment: Computer Conferencing in Higher Education. The Internet and Higher Education 2 (2–3), 1–19.

Gladwell, M. (2001) The Tipping Point: How Little Things Can Make a Big Difference. Little, Brown and Company.

Glatt, T. (ed.) (2002). E-Learning im Spannungsfeld von Potenzial und Realitaet – eine Einführung; In: Autorengruppe E-Writing.de: E-Learning und E-Kooperation in der Praxis (S. I–XXXII). Hermann Luchterhand Verlag.

Haken, H. (1983) Synergetics, an Introduction: Nonequilibrium Phase Transitions and Self-Organization in Physics, Chemistry, and Biology. Springer.

Hersey, P., K.H. Blanchard (1969) Management of Organizational Behavior – Utilizing Human Resources. Prentice Hall.

Hildebrandt, M., V. Gäessler (2001) Role Plays for consultants. Credit Suisse.

Hildebrandt, M., L. Jehle, S. Meister, S. Skoruppa (2013) Closeness at a Distance: Leading Virtual Groups to High Performance. Libri Publishing.

House, R., P. Hanges, M. Javidan (2004) Culture, Leadership, and Organizations: The Globe Study of 62 Societies. Sage.

Herrero, L. (2008) Viral Change: The Alternative to Slow, Painful and Unsuccessful Management of Change in Organisations. Chalfont Project T/a Meeting Minds Publishing.

Ishikawa, K. (2012) Introduction to Quality Control. Chapman & Hall.

Jehle, L. (2015) Wie Sie eine lebendige Gespräechskultur im virtuellen Projektteam etablieren. Projekt Magazin, 15/2015.

Kim, A. J. (2006) Community Building on the Web: Secret Strategies for Successful Online Communities.

Kutz, M. (2008) Toward a Conceptual Model of Contextual Intelligence: A Transferable Leadership Construct. Leadership Review, Vol. 8, 2008.

Lipnack, J., Stamp, J. (2000) Virtual Teams: People Working Across Boundaries with Technology. John Wiley & Sons.

Lojesky, K. S., Reilly, R. R. (2008) Uniting the Virtual Workforce: Transforming Leadership and Innovation in the Globally Integrated Enterprise. John Wiley & Sons.

Luhmann, N. (1987) Soziale Systeme: Grundriss einer allgemeinen Theorie. Suhrkamp.

Majchrzak, A., A. Malhotra, J. Stamps, J. Lipnack (2004) Can Absence Make a Team Grow Stronger? Harvard Business Review 82 (5).

Mandelbrot, B. (2010) The Fractal Geometry of Nature. W.H. Freeman.

Mayo, A., N. Nohria (2005) In Their Time: The Greatest Business Leaders of the 20th Century. Harvard Business School Press.

McLuhan, M. (1964) Understanding Media. The Extensions of Man. McGraw-Hill.

Meyer, E. (2014) The Culture Map: Decoding How People Think and Get Things Done in a Global World. Publicaffairs.

Pagano, K.O. (2014) Immersive Learning: Designing for Authentic Practice. ASTD.

Parker, A. (2003) The Blink of an Eye: The Cause of the Most Dramatic Event in the History of Life. Free Press.

Richter, K., J.M. Rost (2004) Komplexe Systeme. Fischer.

Schweizer, K., M. Paechter, and B. Weidenmann (2001) A Field Study on Distance Education and Communication: Experiences of a Virtual Tutor. Journal of Computer-Mediated Communication, Volume 6, Issue 2.

Röettgers-Ferchland, E. (2008) Wie Columbus Indien fand – oder die Kunst ein Projekt zu vollenden. Profile – Politik, Gesellschaft und Beratung, Nr. 15, 2008.

Rosenberg, M.B. (2003) Nonviolent Communication: A Language of Life. Puddledancer Press.

Schaetti, B.F., S.J. Ramsey, G.C. Watanabe (2008) Making a World of Difference: Personal Leadership. A Methodology of Two Principles and Six Practices. FlyingKite Publications.

Scheuermann, J., M. Hildebrandt (2015) OPR – Optimierung, Polaritäet, Resonanz und Rahmenbedingungen: Organisationsinterne Dynamiken für nachhaltige Veraenderungen nutzen. In: Kantelberg, K., V. Speidel (ed.) Change-Management an Schulen. Carl Link.

Storch, M. (2012) Das Geheimnis kluger Entscheidungen. Piper.

Trompenaars, F., C. Hampden-Turner (2004) Managing People across Cultures. Capstone.

Weick, K.E. (2015) Managing the Unexpected: Sustained Performance in a Complex World. John Wiley & Sons.

Wenger, E. (1998) Communities of Practice: Learning, Meaning, and Identity. Cambridge University Press.

Online resources

http://www.business-leadership-qualities.com

http://community.lithium.com/t5/Science-of-Social-blog/Community-vs-Social-Network/ba-p/5283

http://www.deepdemocracyinstitute.org/deep-democracy-explained.html

Dennett, Daniel C.; Roy, Deb (2015) Wie digitale Transparenz die Welt verändert. Spektrum der Wissenschaft, 6/2015

http://www.spektrum.de/news/wie-digitale-transparenz-die-welt-veraendert/1347106

http://www.forbes.com/sites/lbsbusinessstrategyreview/2014/02/07/developing-contextual-leaders/

www.immersive-coaching.com

Lewis, Myrna: Inside the No, http://www.deep-democracy.net

http://www.paulwatzlawick.de/axiome.html

http://www.pnas.org/content/110/12/4470.abstract

http://www.stevepavlina.com/articles/list-of-values.htm

http://www.uni-graz.at/~huber/ahlectures/content/lecture01/img/energyInput_waterSurface.jpg

http://upload.wikimedia.org/wikipedia/commons/thumb/c/cb/Paramecium.jpg/220px-Paramecium.jpg

http://www.value-test.com/

http://wordnetweb.princeton.edu/perl/webwn?s=intelligence&sub=Search+WordNet&o2=&o0=1&o8=1&o1=1&o7=&o5=&o9=&o6=&o3=&o4=&h=

About the brains behind the book

Line Jehle is founder and Managing Director of perform-globally.com GmbH. She has been working internationally as Executive Coach and Consultant for the past 19 years. The focus of her activities is performing globally. This includes executive training courses, support of international and virtual teams, executive coaching, facilitating and consulting for international enterprises. Because of her Danish heritage and time spent living and working abroad, Line has directly felt and experienced the influences of different cultures. She is keynote speaker at international conferences and lecturer at the MBA Course "International Project Management". Line co-developed the Virtual Performance Assessment (VPA©), a tool that helps professionals understand how they can improve the performance of global teams, groups, and networks. She is co-author of "Closeness at a Distance: Leading Virtual Groups to High Performance". Line is a member of the International Coaching Federation.

Line Jehle

Marcus
Hildebrandt

Dr. Marcus Hildebrandt is founder and Managing Director of learning.de, proSchule.org and head of Virtual Performance Improvement (VPI®) at intercultures.

Marcus has been working internationally – China, Europe, India, North-Africa, North-America and Russia – as an executive coach and consultant in the fields of Personnel Development, Leadership Development, and Organization Development. He has created innovative learning, coaching and meeting formats for the past 18 years. A physicist by training, he has done pioneering work on virtual teams, and on e-coaching (immersive Coaching® and e-moderation. He co-developed the Virtual Performance Assessment (VPA®) and the Feedback Profiler®, two tools that help professionals to improve the performance of global teams, groups, and networks/communities. Inspired by his knowledge of non-linear systems in physics he co-developed a new approach in organizational development based on the inner dynamics of systems and the principle of self-organization: Optimization-Polarity-Resonance (OPR). Marcus is regularly invited to give lectures and courses at different universities and Management Schools. He can be reached at info@marcushildebrandt.de and the same site gives an overview over his current activities: www.marcushildebrandt.de.

Stefan Meister

For 25 years, **Stefan Meister** has supported professionals, teams, and organizations to work better in global complexity. He has done this in his practice as a consultant, trainer, facilitator, and coach, but also through the international consultancy company intercultures, for which he serves as Managing Director.

One of his main areas of expertise lies in improving the performance of virtual teams. He is the co-author of "Closeness at a Distance", a book about high performance in virtual collaboration, the co-developer of the online-assessment tools "Virtual Performance Assessment (VPA)®" and "Feedback Profiler®", and the service portfolio of "Meeting Culture®", which improves meetings at international interfaces.

In the course of his career, Stefan Meister has consulted with and in over 70 international companies in over 30 different countries. He regularly works with and in diversity in Asia, the Americas, the Middle East and Europe and in that great possibility of virtual space, trying to co-create teams, projects, and organizations people want to belong to.